A MILLION MIRACLES

AND THE ONE THAT NEVER CAME

KELCI JAGER

Copyright

Disclaimer

This book chronicles my husband's cancer journey through my very personal journal entries. While it confronts the sensitive topics of serious illness and loss, it ultimately stands as a testament to enduring love, unwavering faith, and the resilience of the human spirit in the face of life's greatest challenges. To protect privacy, some names and identifying details of people and places have been changed. Thank you.

DEDICATED TO

My husband Collin,

You never gave up hope and never stopped fighting for me, our children, and our family.

Your courage inspires me every day. I promise to continue the legacy we started.

Table of Contents

Introduction

Reflecting on my childhood brings a flood of magical memories. I am fortunate to have grown up in a quiet beach town just outside of Los Angeles, California, where I could spend my days immersed in sand, salt, and sun.

I wasn't one to shy away from getting my hands dirty, in fact, quite the opposite. Unconventional pets like skunks and opossums were part of our household, and I took pride in my ability to catch lizards and create habitats for wild frogs. I spent my days exploring every nook and cranny of our neighborhood, and the world felt like my own personal playground.

Growing up as the youngest of six siblings taught me a thing or two about navigating life with a mix of boldness and caution. I was like a curious observer, witnessing the success and trials of my four older brothers and my sister. Through their experiences, I learned a valuable lesson: While we can choose our actions, we can't always control our circumstances. It was a realization that shaped my outlook on life from an early age, teaching me to approach challenges with resilience and adaptability.

Some may have labeled me a tomboy, but I was just as comfortable slipping into a dress and painting my fingernails as I was digging in the dirt.

My best friend lived across the street, and together, we were an unstoppable duo, always on the lookout for our next adventure. On days off from school, we'd wake up early, ready to dive headfirst into whatever mischief awaited us.

The carefree days of my childhood shaped me in more ways than I can count. They instilled in me a sense of independence, confidence, and wonder. I learned to appreciate the beauty of the world around me. And while life may have changed since then, I will cherish the memories of those magical childhood days forever.

When I graduated from high school, I ventured 120 miles south to attend San Diego State University to get my degree in nursing. San Diego had a special surprise waiting for me - my husband, Collin.

Collin grew up as the middle child of five siblings on the salty shores of San Diego, California. Collin, a natural-born athlete, excelled in team sports like basketball, baseball, and football. By the age of 12, standing tall at an impressive 5'11", Collin's athletic prowess caught the attention of the media when he shattered a 30-year-old home run record in Little League, a remarkable achievement that people in his hometown still talk about today.

His talent continued to shine brightly, earning him the prestigious title of All-American at just 14 years old during the AAU Baseball Nationals, along with a gold medal in the Junior Olympics. A series of injuries and surgeries during high school hindered Collin's promising sports trajectory, dashing his hopes of pursuing his athletic dreams. As his path had taken an unexpected turn, fate intervened in a different way. In 1999, our paths crossed, and we quickly fell head over heels in love.

The first time I laid eyes on Collin was at a young adult dance sponsored by our church. I was instantly smitten; he was so darn handsome! At the time I was living in a house with five other girls, I was well-connected socially and recognized him as someone new. Since we didn't know his name, we named him "Red Shirt" due to him wearing a red shirt. Throughout the night, other girls constantly surrounded him. Despite my intrigue, I wasn't keen on competing for his attention, so unfortunately, we didn't get a chance to meet that night.

The following weekend, I attended another young adult church activity, secretly hoping Collin would be there. As I walked into the church, I turned to my friend and whispered, "I hope Red Shirt will be here tonight." Just as the words left my mouth, my heart skipped a beat as I spotted him. Determined to finally meet him, I mustered up the courage and struck up a conversation. During our chat, I mentioned to him that my roommates and I were moving out of our home the following weekend. Little did I know, he saw this as an opportunity to make a move of his own. He offered to help us with the move but later confessed that it was merely a ploy to get my phone number.

Many years later, he wrote me a letter, and he recounted the night we first met. He said, "From the moment I first laid eyes on you, I knew you were special. Besides your beauty, your smile was so inviting. I was drawn to you. Being as shy as I was, I couldn't bring myself over for an introduction. I remember those moments when our eyes would meet, and for me, time stood still during those seconds our gazes locked. Then you came over and talked to me! It was game over; you captivated me. I was so excited to help you and your roommates move. My stomach was full of butterflies as I got to spend that time being close to you. I was hopeful that you'd want to see me again."

Four years later, in 2003, we were married. We were just kids then, at 21 and 23 years old, but we had dreams of building a beautiful life together, and that's exactly what we set out to do.

A year and a half into our marriage, we welcomed our oldest son, Ian. Collin was over the moon with love for our tiny bundle of joy, but as a new dad, he had much to learn. I remember the hilarious mishap of asking him to apply baby lotion to Ian's chapped cheeks, only for him to use diaper rash cream instead. Picture this: our newborn's face coated in thick white cream, leaving Collin utterly perplexed while I burst into laughter.

True to Collin's nature, he quickly adapted and became a parenting pro. Two years later, our family grew with the addition of our son, Lucah. Three years after that, we welcomed our third son, Elijah, and, completing our family, our youngest son Maddox, arrived as the caboose in 2013. There was nothing in this world that Collin loved more than being a father. From the moment our sons entered this life, Collin's purpose became obvious: to be their rock, their mentor, and their steadfast companion. Everything he did, and every choice he made, revolved around our sons. He was a very involved parent, from coaching the boys' sports teams to sharing his love for the ocean with them. One of Collin's favorite things to do was take our children out on his surfboard when they were young; he would ride on the back of the board and allow them to feel the movement of the wave. Once they were strong enough swimmers and could tackle the waves on their own, Collin would give up his surf time to push our children into the waves.

Without a doubt, he played the role of the "fun" parent, and the boys quickly learned that their chances of receiving something they wanted were much higher if they approached Dad. He taught the boys how to catch a ball and how to make a basket; he taught them how to be team players and show good sportsmanship. He taught them how to work and be responsible. He taught them to be gentlemen and how to serve others. He taught them the importance of honesty and integrity. He taught them how to be leaders, good friends, and how to have courage and unwavering faith. He taught them how to be dedicated husbands and provide a stable, unconditionally loving home. Of all the things Collin has taught our boys, the most important is to love God. Collin loves the Lord with all his heart and with an unwavering commitment to serve Him.

It's safe to say, the boys and I hit the husband/father jackpot! Although our lives were not without their challenges, Collin and I remained deeply in love and steadfastly committed to each other and our family. In our little familiarity bubble, we had relocated to the same peaceful town where I had grown up, with our children attending the same schools as I once did. Collin and I had built a successful business together, allowing us to spend most of our days working and playing side by side.

We had created a beautiful life for ourselves, and the thought of ever leaving our little sanctuary never crossed our minds–until one day, when we both felt a sudden and intense prompting that we needed to move to Florida. It came out of nowhere, catching us completely off guard. We had no connections in Florida and no rational explanation for such a drastic move. It took enormous amounts of faith, but within three weeks of the prompting, we were on a plane to look at Florida real estate. It was on that first trip that we bought our home. We were extremely nervous, and everyone back in California told us we were nuts (and honestly, we kind of agreed with them). But we couldn't deny the path that was clearly being marked before us, and even though it was scary, it just felt right.

Our family moved to Florida in December 2019, just a few short months before the COVID-19 pandemic. While the world was in chaos, we were adjusting to our new life in Florida. One stormy night in August 2020, our two oldest sons, Ian (age 15) and Lucah (age 13) were out in the neighborhood with friends. They had stopped at the neighborhood pool with their buddies and called to tell me they were only about five minutes away, and they would soon be home.

After I hung up the phone, I headed to my room to get ready for bed. Soon after, I heard the usual commotion of the boys returning home. However, I quickly realized that the noise I heard was anything but normal; I sensed panic and terror. Collin's urgent voice cut through the chaos, demanding my immediate attention. Without a second thought, I ran out of my room and followed Collin out the front door of our home.

As I rounded the corner of our driveway, my heart dropped at the sight before me. I saw the boys' vehicle lying overturned just a few feet away. The scene was one of chaos and devastation. Shattered glass and debris littered the pavement, and amidst the chaos, Lucah stood slumped over, crying out in pain. Instinctively, my nursing skills kicked in, and I began assessing each child's injuries one by one.

There were six passengers in the vehicle, and Lucah's condition was the most severe. Despite the darkness, I could see the road rash covering the left side of his body, his left arm mangled, and his other arm struggling to support it. Meanwhile, Collin was frantically working to free the passengers trapped by their seatbelts.

Within minutes, the parents of the other passengers arrived, and I knew I had to get Lucah to the hospital immediately. Ian, despite his protests about being fine, revealed that he had hit his head. With no time to spare, I insisted he come with us to the hospital. As we drove to the hospital, Ian began experiencing symptoms of a head injury. He was confused, sensitive to lights and sounds, and began vomiting. Lucah's cries of pain filled the car. I was terrified.

Because of pandemic restrictions, the hospital only allowed one parent to enter. I accompanied Lucah and Ian while Collin stayed behind at home with our younger sons, Elijah (age 11) and Maddox (age 7), anxiously awaiting news of the boy's condition.

The emergency room staff put both boys into one room so I could be with them at the same time. The doctor came into the room, looked at Ian, and said, "I'm not as worried about you as I am about your brother, so I'm going to take care of him first." Soon after, a radiology technician came into the room and took Lucah to imaging, and then they returned for Ian. I was a ball of nerves as I sat alone in the small, cold emergency room and waited to hear the extent of my son's injuries.

Even though the pandemic had restricted our new social life in Florida, we had made some friends. One of those friends was Will, a radiologist at the children's hospital where my boys were being treated. It was late—about 10:30 pm and I did not think that Will would be working or even awake. But I sent him a text message anyway: "Hi Will, not sure if you're on-call tonight, but Ian and Lucah were in an accident. We are in the ER now, and they are getting x-rays and scans taken as I text this.

Do you think you could look at their images and let me know what you see?"

To my surprise, he immediately texted back: "Kelci, I'm not working tonight. But I have access to see all diagnostic pictures from my home. I'll look right now and let you know." Not even five minutes went by, and my phone rang. It was Will. He explained the bones Lucah had broken and told me he would require surgery. Will's next question made my stomach drop. "Has Ian ever had a scan of his brain?" I immediately knew something was seriously wrong. I replied, "No, why?" Will calmly said, "He has a 2-inch brain tumor in his right frontal lobe." Those words sent chills up my spine. My mind started racing with a hundred different thoughts. What? How? But there have been no signs, no symptoms; he is a totally healthy and active kid!

I immediately dialed Collin to give him an update, the shock and anguish were evident in every word I spoke. They hurried Lucah into surgery to reset his broken bones, and Ian awaited brain surgery. The situation was grave.

An overwhelming sense of tension and urgency filled the sights and sounds of this night. The beeping of machines, the hurried footsteps of medical staff, and the whispered conversations between doctors painted a picture of unpredictability and fear. A whirlwind of emotions overwhelmed me, devastation, confusion, and profound shock.

Uncertainty and challenges characterized the following months. The pain from Lucah's injuries weighed heavily on him, but he showed incredible determination and perseverance throughout his rehabilitation journey. He endured three surgeries and months of physical therapy. With each session of therapy, he slowly but steadily regained strength and mobility. After about a year of hard work, he regained 95% of his range of motion and full use of his arm once again.

To remove the tumor from Ian's brain, he underwent a bi-frontal craniotomy, a complex surgical procedure that required the neurosurgeon to make an incision from ear to ear across the frontal portion of the skull. The procedure required meticulous precision and expertise as the neurosurgeon carefully navigated through delicate brain tissue to access and remove the tumor. As Ian bravely faced this challenging surgery, we hoped and prayed for a successful outcome. We entrusted his care to his medical team, knowing that every moment of this procedure was crucial in his fight against this tumor threatening his young life.

Thankfully, the neurosurgeon's skillful hands were able to remove the entire tumor from Ian's brain. However, the excruciating task of awaiting the tumor pathology results tempered our relief. It felt like an eternity during the two-week waiting period.

There are no words to convey the depth of fear and anguish that consumed us during that time. It was a relentless battle against the fear of the unknown as we anxiously awaited the results that would determine our son's future.

Looking back, I can safely say that those two weeks were some of the longest and most agonizing of my life. Yet, amidst the darkness of uncertainty, Collin and I clung to hope and leaned on each other for strength, praying for the best possible outcome for our son.

I wrote these words in my journal: "Today Ian's oncologist called and said all tests on the brain tumor have come to the same conclusion. The brain tumor is benign! And good news! Since the surgeon removed the whole tumor, no chemotherapy or radiation is required.

When the doctor told me this, I dropped to my knees and wept! The refiner's fire sucks! But it is so incredible how my faith has grown stronger. There were times when I felt angels carrying me, as there was no way I could have gotten through on my own.

I have no doubt we have had angels on both sides of heaven tending to our family. I just feel so blessed; there have been so many tender mercies and miracles. The Lord has made Himself known to me! Through Him, I have found peace and healing during a time when I felt like the world was crumbling."

As traumatic as the accident was, and as much pain Lucah had to endure, I can't help but believe that it was meant to happen. Out of the six vehicle passengers, Ian was the only one who hit his head, prompting a head scan because of his injuries. If Lucah hadn't suffered such severe injuries, maybe I wouldn't have taken Ian to the emergency room that night. It was during the peak of the pandemic, and being in a germ-filled emergency room was the last place I wanted to be. The accident occurred late at night; I was tired, and we had friends flying into town to visit us the next day. Ian assured me he felt okay. Who knows, maybe I could have been persuaded to postpone seeking medical attention. The way the accident happened was not coincidental. It was very much a miraculous blessing.

If the accident had not happened in the way it did, perhaps Ian's brain tumor would have gone undetected until it had reached a more critical stage. This thought makes me shudder. I believe the accident was a blessing in disguise. After successfully removing the tumor from Ian's brain, his neurosurgeon said, "I feel so bad that your other son is suffering, but that accident probably saved Ian's life."

Approximately four months following the accident, things were finally beginning to settle down. Ian and Lucah were making steady recoveries and had returned to school, and we were eager to get back to our normal routine. Despite the whirlwind of events—the cross-country move, the boys' accident, and Ian's brain tumor—I was feeling confident in my ability to navigate life's toughest challenges.

Yet, unbeknownst to me, another storm loomed on the horizon, and that confidence I fought so hard to gain was about to be shattered into a million pieces.

Chapter One

The Story Begins...

Day 1
January 2, 2021

For the past few weeks, Collin has been experiencing intermittent chest pain. Initially, we thought little of it, assuming it was costochondritis from a heavy chest workout. Being averse to doctor visits, he managed the discomfort with Tylenol and Motrin. My concern grew when he spiked a fever two days ago, on New Year's Eve, and his pain intensified.

Because it was Saturday and his primary care doctor's office was closed, I suggested he go to the hospital. To ease my worry, he reluctantly agreed to go to the emergency room. Though I offered to accompany him, he insisted he would not be gone long. With a quick kiss goodbye, he headed out the door.

Once he arrived at the hospital, he sent me a text: "Hey, Babe. I got lucky, and they took me back to see the doctor right away. The doctor just ordered some blood work and a few other tests. I shouldn't be here long. Love you!"

A few hours passed, and I received no more updates. Getting worried, I sent Collin a quick text to see how things were progressing. When I received no response,

I called him, but he did not answer. I tried to remain composed, but a sense of panic crept in as I felt that something was wrong. I called the hospital and asked to be transferred to the emergency room.

A few minutes later, I had his nurse on the line. She sounded relieved that I had called, as she explained, "Collin didn't provide any emergency contact information on his check-in form, so we had no way to reach you. When he first got here, we expected he would have a quick visit. But his condition deteriorated rapidly. He spiked a fever of 104 and is experiencing severe chest pain. So far, none of the test results are showing anything too alarming. However, the doctor has admitted him to the hospital until we can determine the cause. Visiting hours are over for today, but you're welcome to come first thing in the morning."

As I sit here at home, alone, my stomach churns with anxiety, and I feel myself being pulled into a dark abyss of fear and dread. It's a familiar sensation, one I experienced the night of the boys' accident. How did things escalate so rapidly? I wish Collin had allowed me to accompany him. I wish he had sought help sooner. Why didn't he provide emergency contact information? I feel overwhelmed with thoughts and questions, which are adding to my growing sense of confusion and frustration.

The harsh reality of this situation sinks in, and my emotions become a tumultuous whirlwind. Fear, anger, and disbelief—each emotion battles for dominance. I try to push aside the dark thoughts, hoping for a night of restful sleep. I pray that tomorrow will bring some answers.

Day 2
January 3, 2021

I arrived at the hospital promptly at 8:00 am this morning, the start of visiting hours. Because of the COVID-19 restrictions, the hospital only permits one visitor per day. Collin looks pale and exhausted. The doctors are puzzled; they suspect sepsis, but the exact source of the infection remains elusive. The nurse took blood cultures last night, but we won't receive results for a few days.

So far, the only abnormalities detected are in his lab results. His blood work shows an elevated white blood cell count and inflammation markers, and his platelet count is low. Despite experiencing intense chest pain, his cardiac labs, EKG, and echocardiogram all came back normal. In addition, the CT scan showed nothing concerning, and his gallbladder ultrasound looked good. Additional tests, including abdominal and chest MRI scans, were conducted today, but we are still waiting for the doctor to share those findings.

Multiple doctors examined him today, each one specializing in something different, and not one seems to know what the underlying cause of his illness is. I'm feeling incredibly overwhelmed. Lucah has another surgery scheduled for his arm on Wednesday, and Ian has a follow-up brain MRI on the same day. With no family here in Florida, I'm struggling with a sense of isolation. How am I going to manage all of these appointments and responsibilities? Thankfully, Collin's mom just booked a flight and will arrive on Tuesday night. Her presence will be a tremendous relief, and I am grateful for the support.

Day 3
January 4, 2021

Today brought more questions than answers. Despite conducting many tests, we still don't know what the problem is. Collin's abdominal MRI revealed an enlarged spleen, which points to infection, but the blood cultures have shown no growth. The medical team is now considering whether this could be a complication stemming from the COVID-19 infection Collin had a few months ago. As the internal medicine doctor put it, "We just don't know what is going on with him; he is just a big question mark."

The doctor's words were far from comforting, especially given Collin's ongoing pain and fever without a clear diagnosis. I am terrified that something might be seriously wrong, but I can feel the strength of the many prayers being said for us. We have received so many encouraging messages from family and friends. This has given me strength and lifted my spirits.

Day 4
January 5, 2021

Our situation remains unchanged, with few answers in sight. Today, the internal medicine doctor said, "You are currently our most complex patient. We have thrown the book at you, and we still don't know what is making you sick!"

What are we supposed to make of a comment like this? Is Collin supposed to wear this as a badge of honor? I'm frustrated and worried. And doctors making statements like this do not bring me any reassurance.

The trauma from Lucah's injuries and Ian's brain tumor weigh heavily on my mind, and I constantly battle worst-case scenarios. Despite my efforts to reign in my imagination, it seems to have a mind of its own, leading me down rabbit holes of possibilities. With my medical knowledge, I feel like I know too much, and it's a constant struggle to stay grounded in the facts. Sometimes ignorance really is bliss.

I can't shake this gut feeling that something more significant is going on here. I pray I'm wrong.

Day 5
January 6, 2021

Collin's illness remains a mystery. We have eliminated several potential causes and narrowed down the possibilities, but he is still very sick, and no one seems to know why. Despite the ongoing investigation, the medical team continues to believe that a viral infection is the most probable cause. But with no definitive test results, we can't just assume it's a virus. I am thankful for our infectious disease specialist, Dr. Eze. He has been incredibly thorough. If there is a virus to uncover, I am certain he will find it.

Today, Dr. Eze ordered a multitude of obscure blood tests in search of potential sources of infection; he is testing for things I've never even heard of. Even Collin's nurse was confused. She had to consult the lab to determine which blood tubes to use for these specific tests. Surprisingly, even the lab technicians didn't know. They had to research the tests to answer the nurse's questions. Dr. Eze is leaving no stone unturned in pursuit of answers.

Meanwhile, specialists from other fields like gastrointestinal and cardiology continue to test for other possibilities. The uncertainty about Collin's condition weighs heavily on us, but we're not navigating this alone. The support of our community has overwhelmed me. Neighbors and friends have stepped up to help with the kids, bring over meals, and even clean the house. Their kindness reminds me of the warmth of compassion and the strength we find in unity.

Day 7
January 8, 2021

Collin has now spent a week in the hospital, and each night leaving him there alone is incredibly difficult. I long for him to be back home with us. Today, the internal medicine doctor mentioned the possibility of Collin being discharged either today or tomorrow. While Collin seemed excited about the prospect, I'm not entirely convinced that he's stable enough to come home just yet. I expressed my worries and insisted on consulting an oncologist, as we haven't yet received their perspective on Collin's condition.

A few hours later, Dr. Patel from oncology arrived to assess Collin's condition. I had a conversation with her, expressing my concerns. With a calm assurance, she shared, "I don't believe this is cancer. All indications suggest an infection. We'll proceed with discharging Mr. Jager today, and he can follow up with me in my office in two weeks. If his labs remain abnormal, then we will do more invasive tests. Your husband has already gone through so much; I don't want to put him through more testing when I don't think that it is necessary."

I understood her reasoning, but I still felt deeply uncomfortable with the proposed discharge plan. I immediately called Dr. Eze, and I told him about my conversations with Dr. Patel and the internal medicine doctor.

His reaction mirrored mine. In a very passionate tone, he said to me, "The other doctors think this is an infection. I'm the infectious disease expert, and this is not an infection! Collin is my patient, and he is not going home until we figure out what is going on. If the oncologist doesn't order the proper tests, I will order them myself. We have not yet tested for blood cancer, and we need to rule it out."

With my background in nursing, Collin's extremely high white blood cell count and extremely low platelet count have led me to consider the possibility of leukemia multiple times. However, I've been pushing these thoughts out of my mind because they are so scary. To me, a leukemia diagnosis is a worst-case scenario. As Dr. Eze spoke those words, a wave of paralyzing fear washed over me. He was confirming my deepest fears as a potential reality, and every fiber of my being longed to escape and deny the nightmare that was unfolding.

A few hours later, Dr. Patel returned to inform me she had ordered two tests: a flow cytometry and a bone marrow biopsy. She clarified that flow cytometry is a blood test used in diagnosing various blood cancers. However, she cautioned that its results are not definitive, and any findings would need to be confirmed with a bone marrow biopsy. Unfortunately, it was too late in the day to proceed with the biopsy, and since it was Friday, we'd have to wait until Monday, as they don't perform that procedure on weekends. Dr. Patel stressed that Collin would need to remain in the hospital until we received these test results.

After another long and exhausting day at the hospital, all I wanted was to come home and spend some time with the boys. I have barely seen them these past seven days, and I miss them terribly. At 9:10 pm, my phone rang. I was upstairs with the boys, snuggled up on the couch, watching America's Got Talent. Worried it might be the hospital calling, I anxiously answered the phone. It was the oncologist, Dr. Patel.

Immediately, I knew something was wrong. Doctors don't call at night for no reason. My hands shook as she asked me if I had a minute to talk. "Yes," my voice choked with emotion, "let me go downstairs to a quiet room." I made my way to my office, and Dr. Patel informed me that one test, the flow cytometry, had come back with abnormalities. She said, "I'm sorry to tell you this, Mrs. Jager. Your husband has acute lymphoblastic leukemia."

Those words hit me like a freight train. I immediately went into shock. My whole body began shaking, and my teeth chattered. It took everything in me to focus on the words that followed. Dr. Patel explained she had spoken to Collin, but she didn't tell him of his diagnosis because he was alone at the hospital.

I went numb, not wanting to believe what she was telling me. Surely, there had been some mistake. I questioned the accuracy of the results, saying, "But you told me the flow cytometry isn't 100% accurate. The results could be wrong." She replied with confidence, "In this case, I am 99% certain the test is correct. We will confirm with a bone marrow biopsy on Monday. I'm so sorry, Mrs. Jager, your husband has cancer."

In disbelief, I hung up the phone, unable to bear the weight of the devastating news alone. My fingers trembled as I dialed Collin's number, tears streaming down my face and my voice quivering with emotion. It was a struggle to articulate the diagnosis through sobs. When I finally managed to get my words out, Collin was also in tears. Despite the overwhelming grief, Collin remained remarkably composed, offering words of reassurance. In that moment, I longed to be by his side, to draw strength from each other's presence. But the hospital's strict COVID-19 protocols meant I couldn't visit after 8:00 pm, leaving me feeling helpless and alone.

Telling the boys was one of the hardest things I've ever had to do. After hanging up with Collin, the weight of that task settled heavily on my shoulders. Climbing back upstairs, I found them on the couch, exactly where I'd left them. How do you shatter your kid's world with such devastating news? I had no script, so through a flood of tears, I just blurted it out. "The doctor just told me Dad has cancer!"

Their expressions froze, disbelief etched across their faces, as my words hung heavy in the air. Their eyes widened, mirroring the shock that gripped their young hearts. It was as though time stood still, every beat of silence echoing the weight of the news. At that moment, I felt their world fracture, the innocence of childhood colliding with the harsh reality of life's unpredictability.

Their questions, so innocent yet profound, highlighted my lack of answers and certainty. We are all a mess, and we are far from okay. When Maddox and Elijah asked to sleep in my bed, I couldn't deny them that comfort. Now, as we lie here together, they're peacefully asleep, but I remain wide awake. My stomach twists with anxiety, a cold sweat breaks out on my skin, and my mind races with relentless, tormenting thoughts. My heart pounds against my chest, and each breath feels like a desperate struggle against an invisible force that threatens to suffocate me.

Day 8
January 9, 2021

The weight of the diagnosis is smothering me. Last night, while Elijah and Maddox slept peacefully next to me, I was wrought with torment. As I wrestled with the harsh reality of our situation, hours slipped away as I delved into research on acute lymphoblastic leukemia. I learned that this aggressive blood cancer, though common in children, is alarmingly rare in adults. The statistics I unearthed painted a bleak picture—the 5-year survival rate hovering at a mere 20-30% for adult patients like Collin.

I am not an oncology nurse, but I have cared for several leukemia patients during my time as a nurse in the pediatric intensive care unit. Some of them survived, but unfortunately, some did not. Leukemia is a cruel and unforgiving disease, and those who battle it endure immense suffering.

One patient remains vivid in my memory—a teenage boy battling leukemia who spent weeks under my care in the pediatric ICU. Tragically, he passed away at the young age of 15, and it happened on my shift. The haunting image of watching his parents say goodbye to their young son has been playing on repeat in my mind.

My tears and thoughts haven't stopped. It feels as if I have been thrown into a deep, dark abyss, with no way to escape. My mind feels enslaved, ensnared by these haunting memories, and I can't stop projecting them

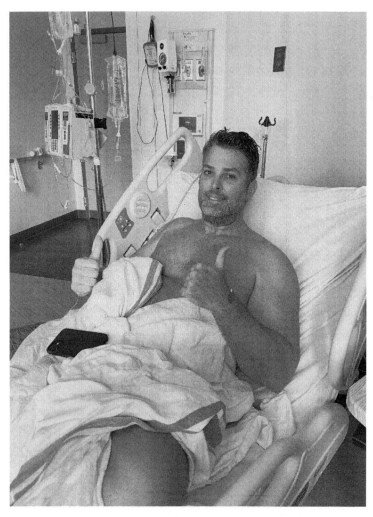

I took this picture of Collin today; when I asked him why he was posing with two thumbs up, with a smile, he said, "Because I am positive everything is going to be okay, I am going to be fine."

onto Collin's future. This torment is unbearable, and I am failing at regaining control.

When I arrived at the hospital this morning, I had hoped that our meeting with the oncologist would bring some assurance and hope. But unfortunately, it did the opposite. Dr. Patel is not working this weekend, so her partner, a general oncologist, came to meet with us. His approach was anything but gentle; he took my anxiety level from a ten to a hundred. He stated that Collin's prognosis is very poor, and without treatment, he will probably survive only a month or two.

Collin's only chance for survival, he explained, will require him to receive a bone marrow transplant. He elaborated that there are four hospitals in Florida with bone marrow transplant programs. One of those hospitals is Southeastern Memorial Hospital, which is located just 30 minutes away. I felt hopeful until he clarified that Southeastern Memorial would not accept Collin as a patient because they do not accept our particular medical insurance.

So basically, what I heard come out of his mouth was, your husband is very sick, and without treatment, he will die very soon. Treatment is available, but it will be denied because he does not have the correct medical insurance.

I was completely shattered, feeling helpless and devastated. My whole body ached as I sat in the chair, sobbing hysterically. The doctor looked me straight in the eyes and said, "Ma'am, I am so sorry. I wish there was more that we could do. Are you a faith-believing woman?" To which I nodded my head. He continued, "Now is the time for you to pray for a miracle."

What? This is your advice? How is this our reality? We just barely picked up the pieces from Lucah's injuries and Ian's brain tumor! And now this? This cannot be happening. Collin is only 39 years old. Please, someone, wake me up from this nightmare!

I definitely spent more time crying today than not. And despite his own fears, Collin spent the day trying to console me. I appreciate how he is attempting to be strong for me. Even in the face of daunting odds, he keeps assuring me, "Babe, I got this!"

I want to believe him, but I am completely overwhelmed and panicked. Collin is my anchor. He is the love of my life, my soulmate, my everything. I am completely devastated. If he doesn't survive, neither will I.

I took this picture of Collin today; when I asked him why he was posing with two thumbs up, with a smile, he said, "Because I am positive everything is going to be okay, I am going to be fine."

Day 9
January 10, 2021

Now I know what it feels like to be in hell. I am currently in hell. The panic attacks won't relent; they're like a vice squeezing the life out of me. My heart races, I can't catch my breath, and my chest is so heavy it feels like it's caving in. Eating and sleeping have become impossible. I can't get my body to stop shaking. I am in deep shock.

Desperately, I seek relief, but the grip of panic refuses to loosen. I try to muster the strength to get out of bed, and be by Collin's side. But, I cannot move. Thankfully, I could send Collin's mom to the hospital today in my place. I can't bear the thought of him being alone.

I haven't stopped praying, pleading with all my heart, begging for a miracle. I am waiting and listening for any sign from God that he hears me, and that He will indeed take this burden away. That He will bless us with a miracle. That He will heal Collin.

But I feel nothing from Him. I feel forsaken. Abandoned. All alone. This sinking feeling only further amplifies my panic and hopelessness.

All that being said, Collin has not lost hope, he has not lost faith, and today he is providing me with a tiny glimmer of light. He sent me and a few members of our family this text message:

"During times of crisis, we need to return to the fundamentals. I am relying heavily on faith, and I pleaded with Heavenly Father last night for a miracle. I asked for a miracle that would show His hand in the healing process so others could see it and know it came from Him.

I can already feel my body changing for the better. I'm experiencing less pain, and my overall well-being has improved!

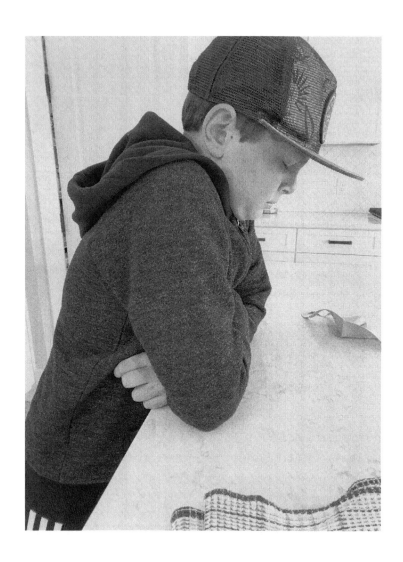

I have experienced many miracles, both small and big, in my life. Let's keep the faith and know that Heavenly Father can grant another miracle for you and me!"

Elijah (age 11 years) also provided me with another tiny glimmer of light today. In our faith, we believe that fasting, coupled with prayer, magnifies our petitions to God. Today, we have people around the world fasting and praying for our family. Elijah wanted to join this worldwide fast for his dad.

At approximately 2:00 pm, with a look of resignation, he turned to me and said, "Mom, I'm so hungry I've got to eat!"

I hugged him tight and told him how proud I was of him for committing to his fast. I secretly snapped this photo of him saying one last prayer to close out his fast. He probably should have taken off his hat, but I think God knows the intent of his heart.

Day 10
January 11, 2021

I'm struggling immensely; I believe I'm experiencing acute stress disorder compounded by trauma from the boys' accident. Never before have I felt such profound despair. It's overwhelming, and I feel utterly defeated.

I desperately need help. Yesterday, I reached out to a psychiatrist via telehealth. It's not ideal, but it was the quickest response I could get on a Sunday. The psychiatrist gave me a prescription for Lexapro: 5 mg for seven days, then increasing to 10 mg. However, it seems like the medication has only worsened my symptoms. Today, I reached out again to another psychiatrist via telehealth, seeking more guidance. They explained that Lexapro can initially worsen symptoms before it improves them. I need to give my body time to adjust to the changes. Praying for my body to adjust quickly, because I hate feeling like this.

It feels like I am spinning out of control, and it is terrifying. I spent the entire night trying to calm my mind and body; I took multiple hot showers and baths, and listened to meditation apps, all while fervently praying for relief. Yet, despite my efforts, nothing is easing my distress.

Adding to my anguish is the heavy burden of guilt I carry because I could not go to the hospital yesterday, and I am unable to muster the strength to go today. Today is an important day; Collin is scheduled for his bone marrow biopsy and PICC line insertion. The PICC line is like a giant IV, which the medical team will use to administer his chemotherapy. It's a temporary IV that they will use until he undergoes surgery to have a port-a-cath surgically inserted under his skin.

While I'm grateful Collin's mom is willing to go to the hospital in my place, I know I should be there. I feel like I'm failing Collin, and our boys. They all desperately need me right now. My desire to be there for them is unparalleled, but I am so depleted. I have nothing to give, mentally, physically, or emotionally. I have never felt so tortured in my life.

I know I need to focus on myself today so that I can pull myself together. Everyone is looking to me to be the rock of our family, but the truth is, Collin is my rock, and without him, I am nothing. Everyone keeps telling me how strong I am. But I am not strong. I am weak. I have crumbled into a million pieces.

Also, I am still trying to figure out how to get Collin accepted as a patient at Southeastern Memorial so he can get the lifesaving treatment he needs. We have a few friends with connections at Southeastern Memorial helping with this task. Since we just missed open enrollment to sign up for a new medical insurance plan, if Collin does get accepted as a patient at Southeastern Memorial, we will have to pay for all of Collin's medical treatments out of pocket. I do not know how we are going to find the money for that, but I am determined to find a way.

Day 11
January 12, 2021

Dr. Patel attempted to initiate a transfer process to Southeastern Memorial today. She was hoping to get Collin admitted for treatment, but when she talked to the other doctor, she received a cold and callous response. The oncologist at Southeastern Memorial, with a dismissive tone, abruptly halted the conversation, stating, "He is self-pay; we can't take him."

The injustice of this is staggering! How is it allowed for someone to be denied life-saving treatment because they don't have the "right" medical insurance? Collin's current oncology doctors are not hematologists. They do not know how to treat leukemia. Without the right treatment, Collin's life expectancy is only weeks to a few months at best, condemning him to a slow and painful death. How is this even allowed to happen in America? How can it be allowed for someone to be denied life-saving treatment if it is available? My brain just is not comprehending!

Everything feels like it's spinning out of control, and I am overwhelmed with fear. Fear for Collin, for myself, and for our boys. The thought of losing Collin terrifies me. I'm terrified of what the future holds for us. My brokenness scares me. I don't know how to put the shattered pieces of myself back together.

As I looked into each of the boys' eyes this morning, I saw the same fear mirrored back at me. It was a wake-up call; I can't let our kids lose both parents. I don't know how to do this, but I must summon every ounce of strength I have left and figure it out.

With this new determination, I forced myself out of bed this morning, and I made it to the hospital. This was so hard because I have zero strength, but I must dig deep and find it. Collin is fighting for me. I will fight for him, and I will fight for our kids.

Collin is developing a rash on his upper extremities and right eye, and he's in a lot of pain from yesterday's bone marrow biopsy; the pain is shooting down his legs. We are anxiously waiting for the biopsy results; I haven't stopped pleading with God for a miracle. For the results to shock everyone, for the doctors to tell us, "We were wrong, there is no leukemia!"

I know the chances of this happening are slim, but I am praying with all the faith I can muster. Of course, Collin remains his optimistic self. He said to me this morning, "I know eventually I will get that miracle. It may not come right away, but that is okay. If I must go through pain to show others God's hand, I will do it!"

I don't understand how he maintains such unwavering faith and conviction. I am fighting with every ounce of energy to keep a positive attitude and an eternal perspective. Despite my relentless efforts, success seems elusive. But I refuse to give up, even when the darkness threatens to consume me.

My friend Peggy tragically lost her daughter, Nicolette, last month. Cancer took Nicolette, a young wife and mom, from this world way too soon. Peggy texted me this today:

"We have a family motto: when you can't see the hand of God in your life, look for His fingerprints. We kept a journal of those fingerprints and added to it every week. The more we acknowledged the miracles, the more we saw, and the more we thanked our Heavenly Father for those miracles, the more He blessed us. Write them down and help your family see them. The spiritual veil will be thin, and your boys will know that God is with you in every step of this journey. This will change you all. How? It is up to you."

These words of encouragement came at the exact time that I needed them, and they have brought me hope. I have been resisting so much of what is. I have been angry with God; I have been bargaining with Him, and I haven't felt Him here. I have screamed at Him, "Why have you forsaken me?"

This message from Peggy has given me hope, and it's given me perspective. It's a beautiful reminder that I need to search for God's fingerprints instead of demanding and telling Him what to do. Instead of focusing on the darkness, I need to look for the light.

Day 12
January 13, 2021

Today, some angels pulled some major strings for us. I have been working tirelessly to get Collin the insurance that he needs so that Southeastern Memorial will accept him as a patient. I have been hitting dead end after dead end, and my efforts seemed futile until some major miracles happened!

I discovered in a very random, roundabout way that my neighbor, who lives about fifteen houses down from us, has just retired from the medical insurance company that we need to get coverage under. With his help and the help of other earthly angels, I was able to get Collin the medical insurance needed to be accepted at Southeastern Memorial as a patient!

I am beyond relieved! The new insurance policy will go into effect in two days, on the 15th! Today, God made

His presence known; what we pulled off today was a miracle.

Since day one of the diagnosis, Collin has been stable and strong. He has maintained a positive attitude and constantly reassures us, "He's got this!"

I am beginning to feel the power of the many prayers being said on our behalf. We are seeing miracles that I know directly result from those prayers!

Trusting in God's timing, I am getting better at keeping an eternal perspective. I have faith that His plan is better than mine, even though sometimes it is hard to see.

Day 13
January 14, 2021

When Southeastern Memorial denied Collin's acceptance as a self-pay patient, it felt like a devastating blow and setback. However, Dr. Patel refused to let this obstacle derail our hopes. Instead, she reached out to Jackson Miller Medical Institute and explained our situation. Miraculously, the hematology team at Jackson Miller agreed to treat Collin and take over care!

Upon learning of Collin's condition, the medical team at Jackson Miller emphasized the urgency of his situation and advised us to bring him there for immediate treatment. Tonight, Collin will be transferred downtown to Jackson Miller Medical Institute. There is no more time to waste; Collin's chemotherapy treatment starts tomorrow.

We feel incredibly blessed. The Jackson Miller Medical Institute is globally recognized for its expertise in treating various forms of cancer, including Collin's disease. While this specific location is relatively new and doesn't yet have a bone marrow transplant program established, its team of highly trained oncologists is renowned for its treatment of hematologic cancers.

As such, our current plan is to start treatment at Jackson Miller. And then, subsequently, when the time is right, their medical team will collaborate with Southeastern Memorial to facilitate Collin's transfer to proceed with a bone marrow transplant.

Chapter Two

Induction Therapy

This is the initial phase of treatment, and it marks the crucial beginning of Collin's treatment journey. These next few weeks are pivotal. Every hour, every dose of medication, and every decision holds the weight of his future. The goal of this induction phase is to achieve remission by rapidly reducing the number of leukemia cells in the body. It involves intensive chemotherapy given over several weeks while being monitored around the clock in the hospital.

We received a warning that the road ahead will be arduous. Collin will receive some of the most potent chemotherapy treatments available. This is a marathon, both physically and mentally, but Collin's got grit, and we've got hope. We are ready to begin the journey back to health, even if we must walk through hell to get there.

Day 14
January 15, 2021

This morning, we met with Collin's new oncology team, and they explained the treatment plan. He will remain in the hospital for at least the next four weeks, receiving in-patient chemotherapy. Dr. Montgomery, the attending oncologist/hematologist, is confident that Collin will tolerate treatment well; he is young, and he is otherwise healthy. Collin's leukemia is B-cell and Philadelphia negative. Leukemia is not staged because of its presence in the blood and bone marrow, it is throughout the body. Instead, doctors assign it a category. However, we don't have all the markers back to give Collin's leukemia a category.

Collin underwent his first chemotherapy session today at noon, marking the beginning of a weekly treatment schedule for the next four weeks, with an additional session scheduled for Monday. Fortunately, he tolerated the treatment relatively well, experiencing only mild nausea, which was effectively managed with anti-nausea medication. However, the treatment left him feeling very fatigued, prompting a two-hour nap afterward. I encouraged him to get up and walk twice; he was very weak and only had the energy to walk for about two to three minutes each time. But he did it; he is such a stud!

Looking ahead, the neuro-oncologist plans to conduct a spinal tap next Friday to test for leukemia cells in the cerebrospinal fluid. During this procedure, the neuro-oncologist will administer chemotherapy directly into the cerebrospinal fluid. This procedure will become a routine part of Collin's ongoing treatment plan. The chemotherapy drugs Collin is receiving come with a range of potential side effects. These include common ones like hair loss, nausea, and vomiting. There's also an increased risk of infection and anemia because of the impact on the immune system and blood cells. He may experience increased susceptibility to bleeding, changes in taste perception, and numbness or tingling sensations in the limbs, known as neuropathy. There are also more serious risks, such as blood clots, particularly in the brain, pancreatitis, and abnormalities in liver function may occur. Because of these potential side effects, Collin will require close monitoring in the hospital throughout this treatment phase.

Day 15
January 16, 2021

Collin woke up this morning feeling much better than yesterday. He said, "I have a lot more energy and I feel good! I'm ready to walk a lot today!" And walk he did! He walked the unit three times for 10-15 minutes each time. Every time he passed the bell hanging on the wall, he said, "I'm going to ring this thing, not today, but I'm going to ring it!"

For Collin, the cancer bell represents more than just the end of treatment—it's a symbol of victory, of triumph over adversity. It's a promise that, no matter how tough the road may be, he will not give up. I can't wait for the day that he gets to ring that bell, declaring to the world that he's beaten this vicious disease.

Today filled me with so much hope. I felt like with each step Collin took, he was reclaiming a piece of himself that cancer had stolen. I am so proud of the determination he continues to show with each challenge he's faced. Today, Collin was the light that shines brightly in the darkness.

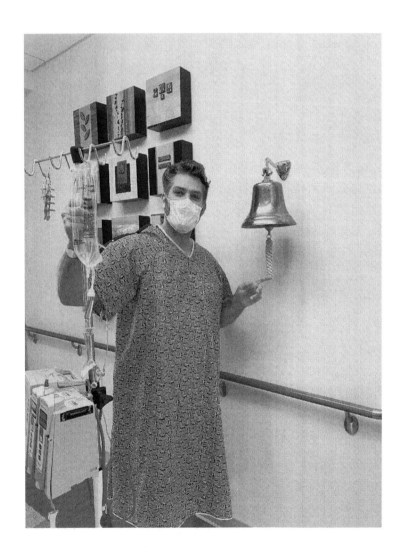

Day 17
January 18, 2021

Collin felt great this weekend. He had more energy and stamina. His pain is being managed with drugs; he looks so much better! Today, he received a very potent chemotherapy drug, pegaspargase. He remains hooked up to a bunch of monitors so they can assess his reaction to this toxic drug. The nurse pre-medicated him with a large dose of IV Benadryl. After a long four-and-a-half-hour nap, he woke up and, aside from feeling tired; he said he felt okay. So far, there are no major side effects from any of the chemotherapy drugs. I'm praying it stays this way.

We continue to count our blessings, but I'm worried about the boys. I hardly get to see them. I spend almost every waking hour at the hospital. Maddox is so young; he is only seven and is having a hard time processing what's happening. He stayed home from school yesterday with a "tummy ache," which was anxiety.

Elijah is also struggling. He's got such a sensitive spirit; last night he told me he prayed and prayed, and the spirit assured him that "Dad would be okay."

Lucah holds everything inside and doesn't show his emotions. I can tell he is nervous and stressed; his worry manifests as hundreds of questions.

Ian is trying to be strong for me, for his brothers, and for Collin despite the immense emotional burden. Every day, he puts on a brave face. It pains me deeply that they have to endure such stress and anxiety at such a young

age. As their mom, I am supposed to protect them, but I can't shield them from this. I wish I had a magic wand that could make all of this disappear.

The kids mirror my feelings closely; when I have moments of panic, they become visibly anxious. Despite the challenges, Collin FaceTimes the boys frequently, which is another tender mercy. For years, he was the only family member with an Android phone. However, he switched to an iPhone just days before falling ill, enabling him to stay connected with the boys through texting and FaceTime.

This has been such a blessing since COVID-19 restrictions have prevented the kids from being able to visit their dad in person. Collin puts on a brave face for our children. They often comment on how "Dad doesn't even seem sick!" Collin gets a little boost of energy every time they call. It's heartwarming and heartbreaking at the same time.

Day 19
January 20, 2021

Today, I gave Collin a haircut. He wasn't quite ready to shave off all his hair, so I just tidied him up a bit. He told me he wanted to look "stealth." The chemotherapy treatment from Monday has taken its toll. He feels fatigued and nauseous. Even sitting in a chair for just 20 minutes for the haircut was a struggle for him. Afterward, he was out of breath while taking a shower, and then he collapsed into his bed. It's devastating to witness him in such a state, knowing that we have a

We took this picture on January 2nd, just hours before Collin's admission to the hospital. It's unbelievable how quickly our lives changed.

long road ahead. I keep reminding myself that this is a marathon, not a sprint.

Day 21
January 22, 2021

We took this picture on January 2nd, just hours before Collin's admission to the hospital. It's unbelievable how quickly our lives changed.

Mostly, Collin is tolerating the chemotherapy treatments. They leave him exhausted and weak; the nurses are doing an excellent job of keeping his nausea under control with medications. He has good days and bad days. Some days he seems almost normal, while other days it's a struggle for him to even sit up in bed.

But even in his fragile state, Collin continues to be "Collin". He continues to embody his compassionate and cheerful spirit, knowing the names of every person who crosses the threshold of his hospital room — from housekeeping to food service, to assistants, to nurses and doctors. He treats every single person who walks into his room with genuine kindness, respect, and appreciation.

Even his doctors marvel at his resilience, noting his enduring smile amid adversity. Countless individuals have expressed to him, "Don't tell anyone else, but you are my favorite patient." His ability to radiate positivity and warmth, even in his weakest moments, serves as an inspiration for all who are around him. How lucky am I that I get to call him mine?

We are hoping he will get to come home for a week-long "break" in early to mid-February before he will need to return to the hospital for more treatment. These past three weeks have been the hardest of my life. I yearn for our old lives when things like exercise, housework, playdates, sports, church activities, and errands were in the list of our priorities. This experience has shaken me to my core. Sometimes I scream and cry at the sky, "Give me my life back!"

I often doubt my ability to handle what is required of me. I don't feel like I am strong enough to carry this burden. Most days, I am confused and scared, and I instinctively try to push away these overwhelming emotions. The pain is paralyzing, and I can't afford to be immobilized. Between endless hours spent at the hospital, the demands of running our business, and the responsibilities of caring for our four children, I feel like I'm drowning under the weight of it all, struggling to keep my head above water as the currents of worry and stress pull me down.

But, despite it all, giving up is not an option. Determined to press forward, I persist by consistently placing one foot in front of the other. Continuing to do my best and show up, I navigate this journey with faith as my compass, focusing on the blessings that illuminate even the darkest of days.

Day 25
January 26, 2021

We received some excellent news this morning: Collin's cerebral spinal fluid came back clean, with no cancer cells detected. This bodes well for his prognosis and means he'll require less spinal chemotherapy. The oncology team is pleased with his progress and remains encouraged by his overall condition.

Today, Collin feels strong. This is a rare occurrence, as the emotional and physical toll of treatment quickly depletes his energy. On days like these, when his strength and spirits are high, I am also surprised by the simplest things he requests. Today it was a shower. Something I take for granted every day is a big undertaking for him. He needs to be disconnected from all the IVs and monitors to shower; so the nurses depend on my presence to supervise and assist him. He is too weak to stand for long, but a shower chair allowed him to sit comfortably for nearly an hour. The warm water washing over him brought him a sense of normalcy and comfort in the clinical confines of the hospital.

In the hospital, time often seems to crawl by slowly. Sometimes, Collin and I will pass the time by watching movies. I always let Collin choose, although I know he'll ultimately defer to me. My go-to genre is comedy—it's a deliberate choice because I love to hear Collin laugh. His laughter has a soothing effect on my soul. Cancer has threatened to steal away so much of our joy. There's something undeniably healing about sharing laughter.

Today, we watched one of Collin's favorite movies, Nacho Libre. It's a movie he's watched countless times with our boys. I'll admit that I have always dismissed it as ridiculous, and I never really gave the movie a chance before. However, today I realized it's hilarious! As we snuggled together in the hospital bed, listening to Collin's laughter fill the room, I found myself genuinely happy. I miss being close to him; I miss feeling connected. Today was a blessing. It brought laughter and light.

Day 26
January 27, 2021

Collin shared a profound experience on the family text thread this morning:

"I had a spiritual experience this morning that I want to share: The hospital environment brings me lots of anxiety, making it hard to sleep. Uncertainty and vulnerability are my constant companions, as my mind races with thoughts of what the future may bring. Early this morning, around 2:00 am, I got some fantastic news that I wouldn't need a blood transfusion today. My hemoglobin jumped from 7.1 g/dl yesterday to 8.6 g/dl today, (the normal range is 13.8 to 17.3 g/dl) and my platelets jumped from 83,000 mcL to 117,000 mcL (the normal range is 150,000 to 450,000 mcL).

With this news, I felt so much gratitude in my heart for the many healing blessings I have received. Feeling the spiritual veil was thin, I sensed my dad and other departed loved ones. I spoke out, asking my dad if he was with me, and he replied that he was here. I asked for others who have passed, including Aunt Jamie, Uncle Cal, Grandma, and Grandpa. Each one answered me, confirming their presence.

I also asked for Nicolette, (our friend who just passed away from cancer in December) who responded quickly and said she was here too. On earth, Nicolette was deaf, but during this experience, I heard her heavenly voice (not her earthly voice). The way she spoke was as clear as day.

Knowing that these people I love were with me caused my soul to experience a deep peace and a flood of tears. Heaven is closer than we think. The love and support of those who have passed on surround us. I know my cancer diagnosis is hard on everyone in our family. I want you to know I love all of you very much!"

Collin has had many spiritual experiences like this since he has been sick. Every time he shares them, my belief in life beyond this mortal world grows stronger. I believe that we have guardian angels guiding, protecting, and blessing us. This belief serves as a deep well of comfort amidst the trials our family faces.

The weight of responsibility I carry right now is massive. Balancing the need to maintain a semblance of normalcy for our boys, ensuring Collin receives optimal care, and remaining strong for everyone to lean on. It's an immense challenge, and there are countless moments when I feel utterly alone in this struggle. Collin's text is a beautiful reminder to me I am never truly alone.

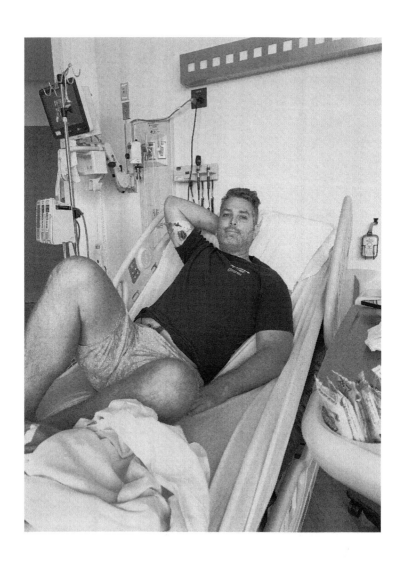

I have heaven's help, and the bonds of love transcend the boundaries of life and death.

Day 27
January 28, 2021

When Collin was first hospitalized earlier this month, I felt a deep desire for him to be ministered to by Elders from our church. With COVID-19 visitor restrictions in place, achieving this seemed like an insurmountable challenge. However, I persisted. Eventually, I persuaded the charge nurse to allow one Elder to come and provide Collin with a blessing of healing and comfort.

During this blessing, several poignant words were spoken: "Ministering to others during this challenging trial will provide you with strength. As you extend care and support to those around you, it will not only be a source of comfort for yourself but also a blessing for those whom you serve."

Initially, I couldn't comprehend how Collin could serve others while battling this disease in the confines of a hospital room. However, I have witnessed this blessing unfold before my eyes in the most beautiful and unexpected ways.

One of our very dear friends, Kristen, in California, sent this text this morning. It touched me deeply:

"Good morning, Collin and Kelci. Do you remember your prayer, Collin, that miracles could happen in your life to show God's power and touch the hearts of others to see His hand?

That happened yesterday. Kelci sweetly shared with me about the special miracle of hearing your guardian angels with you. She must have felt inspired to do that. Last night, I went to visit a family whose husband/ dad died suddenly yesterday from COVID-19. They are in shock and deep grief. When I arrived with food and flowers, they were all gathered on the front lawn having a conversation together. I don't know this family well, and I had planned a drop-and-dash, so I hadn't prepared what I should say to them.

As I stood there with these seven grieving adults, listening for what God would have me say, it came to me to share the experience you had the previous night and share my witness that their husband/father still lives, and they will see him again. As I recounted your story, the Spirit was so strong.

Then, I received the inspiration to ask if I could pray with them and plead for their husband/father to be near them. They agreed, and as I prayed for their family, there was a palpable sense of peace. The wife/mother texted me a few hours later to tell me how deeply impacted they were by this. I honestly don't know if they had ever prayed together as a family before, and it was an incredibly special moment. Thank you for sharing your miracle to strengthen others. You provided a very special gift to a grieving family."

Kristen's experience is a testament to Collin's ability to serve and bless others, even in the confines of his hospital bed. It illuminates how his journey of faith has impacted the lives of individuals in ways we could never have expected. It's a reminder that even amid our trials, we can be instruments of peace and hope for those around us.

Day 32
February 2, 2021

The grueling side effects of chemotherapy are taking a toll on Collin, affecting not only the cancer cells but also his healthy cells. He faces a constant battle with nausea, resulting in significant weight loss and muscle atrophy. His body, once healthy and strong, now feels like a mere shadow of its former self. Even the simplest tasks, like sitting up in bed, are monumental because of his extreme weakness.

With his white blood cell count alarmingly low, Collin is at high risk of infection. Additionally, he has severe anemia and has needed several blood transfusions. And a dangerously low platelet count increases his risk of internal bleeding.

However, the most concerning aspect is the damage inflicted on his liver. Last night, we discovered Collin is suffering from hepatic encephalopathy—a condition where the liver struggles to process waste, leading to a buildup of ammonia in the bloodstream. This toxic accumulation in the brain disrupts normal function, manifesting in confusion, disorientation, and extreme lethargy. In severe cases, it can lead to coma and even death.

Over the past few days, I've noticed Collin becoming increasingly confused and struggling to keep his eyes open. Yesterday, I urged the doctors to conduct neurological tests, which revealed elevated ammonia levels in his bloodstream.

Unfortunately, we have to delay his chemotherapy treatments until his condition stabilizes. We're fervently praying for his body to find strength and healing so he can resume his fight.

Day 33
February 3, 2021

This is gut-wrenching. I'm watching helplessly as Collin's body is deteriorating. His liver levels keep rising, his legs and feet are extremely swollen, and the whites of his eyes have turned a bright yellow. He is very weak and lethargic. I can barely get him to keep his eyes open. He cannot carry on a conversation, and it is difficult for him to get out the words he wants to speak. The doctors suspect that his liver is failing because of the side effects of the chemotherapy drugs.

Unfortunately, we can only monitor his condition and wait with heavy hearts because there are limited treatment options available. On top of this stress, I also worry about the possibility of Ian's brain tumor returning. One of the worst days of my life was when we discovered Ian had a brain tumor. The agonizing wait to determine if it was benign or malignant felt like an eternity.

Conversely, one of the most joyous moments of my life came when his oncologist called with the incredible news that the tumor was non-cancerous. I will never forget the profound gratitude I felt in that moment.

Now, as Ian undergoes another MRI today to check for any signs of recurrence, I cling to that sense of gratitude. It's challenging to articulate the myriad emotions I've experienced over the past five months—moments of devastation juxtaposed with profound awe and wonder. I oscillate between fear of the unknown and overwhelming appreciation for the miracles I've witnessed. This paradox is confusing, but it also makes perfect sense. Right now, I'm pleading for heaven to help me focus on the blessings. Otherwise, my fear will consume me.

Throughout the entire process, Ian has remained remarkably calm and fearless. He shown no signs of worry or displayed even a hint of victimhood. I even wondered if he was in denial, but it's clear that he's just incredibly confident.

As we drove to the hospital today for his scans, I couldn't help but ask if he was nervous. His response was steadfast, "Mom, everything is going to be fine. I am going to be fine. Even if the tumor does come back, we will deal with it. Just like we dealt with it the first time, and just like Dad is dealing with his cancer. No matter what happens, Mom, we can handle it."

I'm not sure where this confidence and wisdom in my 16-year-old son comes from, but I wish I could bottle some of it for myself.

Day 34
February 4, 2021

I have both good news and bad news. The good news is that Ian's brain scans have come back clear, showing no signs of a recurring tumor! His brain appears to be healing well. However, the bad news is that Collin's liver is displaying severe damage. His bilirubin levels are continuing to rise, with today's reading at 15.3 mg/dL (normal range is 0.1 to 1.2 mg/dL). As a result, he cannot proceed with his scheduled chemotherapy tomorrow.

Today has been a rollercoaster of emotions, leaving me torn and conflicted. On the one hand, I feel a tremendous sense of gratitude for Ian's clear brain scans, which has provided a moment to breathe a sigh of relief. But alongside this gratitude comes a wave of concern and worry for Collin's condition. Every time we pause chemotherapy, we give the cancer a chance to gain strength, a terrifying possibility that never leaves my mind. The uncertainty surrounding Collin's liver adds to my trepidation. The doctors cannot predict its trajectory. Will it continue to deteriorate into failure? Or will it suddenly begin healing itself?

The mix of emotions is confusing. While I celebrate Ian's health, I am simultaneously struggling with the harsh reality of Collin's deteriorating condition. Life is so unpredictable, and this unpredictability creates a ton of anxiety for me. I'm trying to find a balance between hope and despair. Ian's progress gives me hope for his continued recovery, but I am simultaneously preparing for the obstacles that lie ahead with Collin's health. It's a delicate dance.

In response to this challenging situation, we have decided to hold a special fast for Collin this Sunday. During this time, we will offer prayers specifically for his body to be strengthened so that he can resume his chemotherapy regimen. We firmly believe in the power of fasting and prayer to invoke spiritual strength and bring about miraculous outcomes. Even amidst setbacks, our faith remains unwavering, and we trust God will continue to bless our family abundantly.

Day 35
February 5, 2021

Caregiver fatigue is real. Collin has now been in the hospital for five weeks! Balancing his care while still attending to the needs of our boys has been extremely difficult. Each day feels like a marathon of emotions, challenges, responsibilities, and decisions. There is no way one could prepare to face this.

I strive to ensure that Collin receives the attention and support he needs while also being present for our children, offering them comfort and reassurance during this unsettling time. But I recognize I am slowly losing myself in this process. I have neglected my well-being and prioritized everyone else's needs above my own. And I'm suffering because of it, I am so exhausted. I have never been this emotionally or physically tired, and I just don't see an end in sight.

Ironically, we took this picture last Halloween, in 2020. Collin as the patient, and me as the caregiver/nurse.

Feeling burned out, I've realized the necessity for change. Moving forward, I intend to prioritize my needs more intentionally, understanding that caring for others hinges on caring for myself first. We have received an outpouring of support from family, friends, neighbors, and even strangers. The love shown to our family has been overwhelming. Initially, I was hesitant to accept help, but I quickly realized I could not shoulder this burden alone.

I am deeply grateful for the help we've received, which has lightened my load and provided strength on the hardest days. Their generosity and kindness humble me and remind me of the importance of community and support during times of struggle.

Day 36
February 6, 2021

Last night, on my way home from the hospital, I stopped at the grocery store to pick up some essentials: The boys need milk for breakfast and bread for sandwiches tomorrow. It is such a normal everyday task, yet it felt so odd in the chaos of my current life.

Walking through the aisles, surrounded by people going about their business, I felt like I was in the twilight zone. Everyone around me seemed to go about their day, oblivious to the fragility of life. With each person I passed, I felt an overwhelming urge to grab their shoulders and enlighten them.

"Don't take anyone or anything for granted; at any moment, it can all be ripped from you!"

It was like a mantra echoing in my mind, a desperate plea born from the rawness of my experience. The faces I passed, lost in their own worlds, seemed oblivious to the fragile nature of existence. If only they knew the pain of having their whole world turned upside down. I am envious of their ignorance.

The beeping register and the friendly cashier asking about my day felt like background noise to the storm raging within me. I wanted to scream, "Can't you see I'm broken? Can't you tell I am suffering? Don't you see that I barely have the strength to put one foot in front of the other?" I wanted to unleash and let out all the pain and fear that has been building up inside me. But instead, I forced a smile and muttered some meaningless response about my day being okay.

Leaving the grocery store, I keep thinking that while my world has come crashing down, life is continuing as normal for everyone else. It made me wonder how many times I have interacted with people who were silently struggling with their own battles, hidden behind masks of normalcy. This thought makes me feel ashamed, so I am committing to myself right now to always be kind and empathetic. For we never really know what someone else may be experiencing. As the saying goes, "You have never walked a mile in another person's shoes," reminding us that each person's journey is unique and filled with unseen struggles.

Day 38
February 7, 2021

Prayers and fasting really work miracles! Yesterday, hundreds of people around the world joined in prayer and fasting for Collin. Today, after 38 days in the hospital, he has stabilized enough to come home!

Collin's white blood cell count has increased. He is still at high risk for infection, but no longer in a critical sense. His platelet count and red blood cell count have also increased enough that they are no longer factors keeping him in the hospital. But his liver is still furious, and the doctors told me yesterday he is in acute liver failure.

Collin has been pleading with the doctors to allow him to come home, yet understandably, the medical team was hesitant because of concerns about his liver. It took some persuasion on my part. I assured them I would monitor him 24/7 and promised to alert them to any concerning developments. Collin's earnest pleas, coupled with our commitment to outpatient clinic visits for labs every morning, eventually convinced them to allow his discharge!

The chemotherapy drug pegaspargase has caused liver damage. It's a very intense and hard-hitting chemo drug that works very well at killing lymphoblastic leukemia cancer cells. But it is also great at damaging the liver. Since this is the cause of the liver damage, there is not much the doctors can do to help the liver heal beyond stopping all chemotherapy and giving the

liver a break. So now we are in a waiting game. There is a possibility the liver will heal itself, but we don't know how extensive the damage is, and there is also a possibility that liver failure will get worse and have fatal consequences.

As we navigate this waiting period, I am pleading for heaven's help. Please bless Collin's liver to heal and for the leukemia to remain subdued.

The severity of his liver failure is apparent; Collin's skin has taken on a pumpkin-orange hue, and the whites of his eyes are bright yellow. He is experiencing significant fluid retention, evident in the swelling of his abdomen, legs, and ankles, which are three to four times their normal size. This buildup of fluid is a consequence of his liver's inability to regulate fluid levels properly. Fortunately, with the aid of medication, the doctors have reduced his ammonia levels, so he no longer has hepatic encephalitis, alleviating his confusion and excessive lethargy.

Leaving the hospital today with him in the car, sitting next to me, was such a surreal moment. Collin was beaming; his smile was broad and beautiful, and I was filled with lots of emotion and gratitude. There have been so many moments during these past 38 days that I didn't think he would leave the hospital alive.

But the best part of today happened when we pulled into our driveway, and all four boys came running out to greet their dad. Because of pandemic restrictions, our sons haven't been able to come visit their father in the hospital. They have not seen each other for 38 days. One by one, the boys each gave Collin a big hug. Collin was sobbing. He missed them so much!

In anticipation of Collin coming home, I wrote words of encouragement on approximately twenty note cards and strategically placed them on mirrors, doors, and cabinets all around the house. The notes say things like "Jager Strong," "You are loved," "Look for the light," "You are the best part of my day," "You are beautiful," "God has not forsaken you," and "You are amazing." When Collin walked into the house, he noticed the notes, and he slowly went from room to room, reading every single note. With tears in his eyes, he looked at me and said, "I didn't know if I was going to make it home. I am so grateful to be home with all of you."

I'd be lying if I pretended I was not fearful of the future, but right now I am relishing this moment. My heart is so full!

Day 39
February 9, 2021

Collin's return home has brought us great joy, and it has significantly lifted both his spirits and ours. My background in nursing has proven invaluable in managing his care at home, which involves administering nineteen different medications daily. Today, we spent five hours at the Jackson Miller outpatient cancer clinic, and Collin was determined to use the walker and wouldn't allow me to push him around in a wheelchair.

At the cancer clinic, we met with Dr. Larson, Collin's outpatient hematologist/oncologist. During our meeting, Dr. Larson discussed Collin's prognosis and reiterated that statistically with treatment Collin has a 30% chance of surviving this year. Of course, I don't like those odds, but he said that he found encouragement in Collin's young age and how well Collin has handled the treatments so far.

Dr. Larson went into detail about his concern for Collin's liver and the fact that we have to pause all chemotherapy treatments until his liver has healed. He clarified that in the past, they only prescribed the drug pegaspargase to pediatric patients with acute lymphoblastic leukemia (ALL), and this is one reason pediatric ALL patients have a better prognosis than adult patients. Pediatric patients can tolerate this drug much better than adults. In recent years, hematologists started treating adult ALL patients under the age of 40 with the pediatric regimen of pegaspargase, and survival rates in those adult patients improved. Unfortunately, Collin's first dose of pegaspargase led to liver failure, which is severely complicating his treatment plan.

The challenge now is to determine the best course of action. Dr. Larson is worried that even if Collin's liver heals, the delay in chemotherapy could give the cancer cells time to regroup and become more resilient. We are fervently praying that the cancer does not gain any momentum during this chemotherapy break and that Collin's liver heals enough for him to resume his next scheduled treatment on February 17, even though it's thirteen days late.

We must weigh the risks and benefits of continuing with the pediatric regimen, which includes more doses of pegaspargase. If Collin's liver heals, the next dose of pegaspargase poses a high risk of liver failure again. If this occurs, the liver may eventually heal, though the recovery could take longer. This delay in treatment could allow the leukemia to progress and become more difficult to treat.

But it is also possible that the liver will handle subsequent doses of pegaspargase. Dr. Larson explained that the initial dose of medication shocks the liver, and subsequent doses may not cause such liver damage. In that scenario, Collin's prognosis would be much better, and his odds of survival would increase by staying with the pediatric regimen and not switching to the adult regimen.

Alternatively, switching to the adult regimen offers a less intense treatment approach. But comes with a diminished prognosis and the necessity of a bone marrow transplant, a challenging process fraught with its own fatal risks.

My head is spinning. I wish we knew the best treatment approach for Collin. Dr. Larson told us we could take a couple of days to think it over before we have to decide. We pray the Lord will give us mental clarity to know what treatment regimen to proceed with. Later this week, Collin has a scheduled bone marrow biopsy to assess the leukemia cell count. If the count is less than 5%, it means that the induction phase of chemotherapy has been successful, and his leukemia will be considered in remission.

Day 40
February 10, 2021

I rely on prescription sleeping medication every night to quiet my anxious mind and allow me to sleep. However, last night, despite taking my medication, I found myself unable to sleep. Instead, I spent the night awake, deep in thought, conducting research, and offering prayers, all in search of clarity regarding the treatment plan for Collin. I am so unsure which regimen is the best way to go, pediatric or adult.

In contrast, Collin woke up this morning with a sense of certainty. He expressed his decision to continue with the pediatric treatment plan, confident in its efficacy. I replied with skepticism and reminded him that if the pegaspargase continues to cause liver failure, his chemotherapy treatments will continue to be delayed. Allowing the cancer cells to increase in strength and numbers. He remained calm and resolute, and with confidence, he reassured me that wouldn't happen.

Collin shared that he had reached out to seven ordained Elders from our church, inviting them to our home to administer a healing blessing tonight. He is confident that this blessing is going to heal his liver and do so at a rapid rate. He believes that the extreme swelling in his

legs will subside, and he will be able to continue with his next scheduled chemotherapy on February 17th.

Again, I replied with skepticism. Being a nurse, I know that while the liver can repair itself, it requires time and doesn't just heal overnight. I believe in Collin's faith and the potential for miracles, yet my realist instincts make me prone to doubt.

Day 41
February 11, 2021

Last night, all seven Elders could come to our home and administer a blessing upon Collin. The presence of the Holy Spirit was palpable, and Collin's unwavering faith was nothing short of incredible. Today, I witnessed an astonishing transformation as his body began to heal itself.

I am utterly amazed to see the tone of his skin return to normal; the jaundiced orange-yellow hue has disappeared. The swelling in his abdomen, legs, ankles, and feet has nearly vanished entirely. Just last night, he exhibited severe pitting edema, with indentations on his skin persisting for over 30 seconds upon pressure. However, by this afternoon, there was no evidence of pitting edema whatsoever!

I am astonished! This is a miracle, and Collin never doubted.

Day 44
February 14, 2021

Celebrating our 21st Valentine's Day together, though certainly not under the best circumstances, reminds me not to take any moment together for granted.

Today, Collin weighed in at 228 lbs, a stark contrast to the 232 lbs he weighed yesterday, and the 242 lbs the day before that. Observing him lose 40 lbs in less than 6 weeks, most of which is muscle mass, is incredibly distressing.

For years, Collin and I have followed a morning routine. We get the boys off to school and then head to the gym together for a workout before diving into our work. Our lives are deeply intertwined; we live, play, and work together. He is present in every part of my day.

I have watched Collin transform from being a healthy, strong, and active individual to frail, weak, and extremely unhealthy. This experience has shattered my heart. There are no words to describe the agony of witnessing someone you love suffer and being utterly helpless to alleviate their pain. I have done everything in my power to control the uncontrollable. Of course, I have been unsuccessful. It has only led to feelings of anger, depression, anxiety, and fear.

I do not have control of this situation, and this reality is devastating and heartbreaking. But now, I am learning to give it all to the Lord because I know He can mend all things that are broken. He is the master healer, and it is only through Him that I find the strength to endure.

Day 45
February 15, 2021

What a difference a week makes, and mighty miracles, of course! We had a follow-up with Dr. Larson today, and we got great news. Collin's liver enzymes are within normal limits, and he's cleared to resume chemotherapy this week. This is such a relief.

Dr. Larson could not believe the progress Collin has made in just 7 days, and he fully supports continuing with the pediatric treatment regimen.

He said, "I can't believe you are the same person I saw last week. You have made remarkable progress!"

Today was extremely encouraging, and Collin is more determined than ever to keep going!

Day 47
February 17, 2021

Today, we received the final pathology report, and there were no leukemia cells detected! Which means that Collin is in remission! This is the best possible outcome we could hope for at this stage. Given the ability of leukemia cells to hide and the aggressive nature of Acute Lymphoblastic Leukemia, Collin will need to continue treatment for the next 2-3 years. While there is still a long road ahead, we express gratitude to God, Jesus Christ, ministering angels, and modern medicine for this remarkable outcome!

Chapter Three

Consolidation Therapy

Following Collin's induction therapy, which marked the initial step in combating his leukemia, we now move on to the next phase of his treatment journey: consolidation therapy. Consolidation therapy will be administered primarily in the outpatient clinic. Collin will face additional rounds of intense chemotherapy, each session aimed at targeting and eliminating any residual cancerous cells that may still linger within his body, reducing the risk of relapse.

As we navigate this phase of treatment, the goal remains clear: to fortify the gains made during induction therapy and pave the way for a future free from the grip of leukemia. This journey is fraught with challenges and uncertainties, but going into this phase, Collin is determined and confident. His unwavering spirit serves as a beacon of strength, reminding me that even in the darkest of times, there is always light to guide us forward. Together, we press on, fortified by the belief that brighter days are ahead.

Day 64
March 6, 2021

This week has been incredibly difficult; truly, it has tested every ounce of our strength. Another round of intense chemo started on Monday, and Collin is feeling the effects of the poison that is constantly being pumped into his body.

When Collin received his leukemia diagnosis 58 days ago, my mind and body shut down. I entered a hopeless realm I had never experienced before—a place I can only describe as hell. I felt so alone and helpless, in complete despair, begging and pleading with God to help my husband, to help me, and to help our family.

While trying to crawl and feel my way out of the darkness, a wise friend counseled me with these words that I will never forget: "Don't forget you're human. It's okay to have a meltdown; just don't unpack and live there. Cry it out, then refocus on where you're headed."

Life is about accepting challenges and choosing to keep moving forward. I will never give up hope because I know all things are working for my good! I am not there yet, but I believe one day I will look back on our journey and thank God for all the pain we endured. For it is through adversity that we gain our courage and strength. No matter my struggles, I will choose joy!

Day 66
March 8, 2021

I found out today that last week Collin overdosed on the chemotherapy drug cytarabine. The prescribed dose for Collin was 75 mg/meter^2, but he received a whopping 375 mg/meter^2 for four consecutive days - Monday through Thursday. The repercussions were immediate. He slept all day Tuesday, Wednesday, Thursday, and Friday.

To say this error enraged me is an understatement. The thought of Collin, already battling through intense chemotherapy, being subjected to such a dangerous mistake is unfathomable. I am consumed with anger, frustration, and fear. How could this happen? How could those entrusted with Collin's care make such a careless mistake?

As we navigate this latest setback, I cling to the hope that justice will prevail, and I expect the proper people will take steps to ensure such a grievous error never happens again. But for now, my focus remains on Collin—his well-being, his strength, and his unwavering spirit in the face of adversity. Together, we'll weather this storm, leaning on each other and drawing strength from our faith.

Day 73
March 15, 2021

Because of the chemotherapy overdose two weeks ago, Dr. Larson skipped Collin's scheduled chemotherapy last week. Collin was not complaining about getting a break. But I'm still really upset about the overdose, and Collin has noticed neuropathy in his fingers. Collin seems to think it's because of the extra chemotherapy he received, but the doctor isn't so sure because he said that isn't a known side effect of cytarabine. I guess we have no way of knowing who is right.

Even though Collin requires a lot of help from me at home, I am so happy that he can receive most of the chemotherapy in this consolidation phase as an outpatient. He despises being in the hospital; I hate going to the hospital, and nothing seems right in the world when he isn't home with me and the boys.

Day 90
April 1, 2021

Last week, Collin received a second dose of pegaspargase, and understandably, we were all on edge about how his liver would react, especially considering his previous experience with liver failure. Dr. Larson reduced the dosage from what he had received previously, and so far, things are looking positive. While his liver enzymes showed a slight increase, it's nothing compared to what happened last time. There might be a slight delay in his upcoming chemotherapy treatments, but fortunately, it's not significant enough to cause concern about the leukemia gaining strength.

Although Collin's liver isn't exactly thrilled about the drug, it's tolerating it, which is a tremendous relief. This means that Collin can keep moving forward with the pediatric regimen!

Day 100
April 11, 2021

One hundred days ago, Collin drove himself to the emergency room, and this nightmare began unfolding before us. That feels like a lifetime ago. Reflecting on the past hundred days feels surreal; it's hard to believe how much our lives have changed in such a short time. A hundred days ago, I couldn't have imagined the challenges we would face.

This phase of treatment is a lot less exciting than the induction phase, which I wholeheartedly welcome. I now crave the mundane and boring. The past eight months have brought enough unwanted adventure to last a lifetime.

Through it all, Collin continues to amaze me with his courage. He faces each dreadful chemotherapy infusion with remarkable bravery, despite knowing full well the toll it will take on his body afterward. It's a rollercoaster ride of emotions and physical burdens. With each infusion, waves of nausea and fatigue inundate Collin, but he experiences a brief respite as he begins to feel better before the cycle repeats once again.

This relentless process weighs heavily on both of us. I wish we could fast-forward through this chapter of our lives to a time when cancer no longer dictates every aspect of our existence. We can't, so I hold on to glimmers of hope and a belief that each day brings us closer to reclaiming normalcy and freedom from this horrific disease.

Day 119
April 30, 2021

Today was a challenging yet hopeful day. Collin's platelet count was critically low this morning, putting him at risk for internal bleeding. I rushed him to the outpatient clinic for a platelet transfusion. As part of her routine questions, the nurse asked, 'Do you ever feel like you want to go to sleep and never wake up?' His response, filled with determination and resilience, warmed my heart. "No, never. I have too much to fight for!"

He truly is a rock star. Every day, I sit back in awe and watch my husband endure the trials of this unfair situation. Even though he has every reason to play the role of victim, I have never heard him ask, "Why me?" Despite the many setbacks he's faced, he keeps pushing forward, refusing to be defeated.

After this week, Collin will get a much-needed chemotherapy break. And then in a few weeks, he will have another bone marrow biopsy. This test will determine if a bone marrow transplant is necessary.

We're praying fervently for results that show no leukemia cells. If Collin can avoid having a transplant, that would be an immense blessing.

Day 127
May 8, 2021

In February, when Collin was still in the hospital, my friend Rosario reached out to me with an incredibly touching gesture. She expressed her desire to support our family and proposed the idea of organizing a 5K race in Collin's honor. Rosario explained that she wanted to find a meaningful way to show our family that we were not alone, despite the physical distance imposed by COVID-19. She believed that hosting a race, Lace Up for Collin, would not only allow our community to come together in support but also reflect Collin's love for the outdoors and active lifestyle.

Her compassion and willingness to take on the responsibility of organizing such an event moved me deeply. She assured me I wouldn't have to worry about a thing; she would handle all the details. With a grateful heart, I accepted her offer.

Today was race day, and the event was truly incredible! The turnout was overwhelming, and the outpouring of support and love profoundly touched our family. Also, I am so happy Collin felt strong enough to attend the event in person.

Meeting so many amazing people at the race was an experience we will never forget. From the 45 dedicated volunteers who worked tirelessly to make the event a success, to the over 250 participants who showed up to run, walk, and support our family, to the 12 generous company sponsors, we felt surrounded by an incredible sense of unity and compassion.

The strength and boost we felt from this show of support is immeasurable. Knowing that so many people came together to rally behind us has filled our hearts with

hope and gratitude. It was a powerful reminder that we are not alone in our journey.

Day 138
May 19, 2021

Collin's body is weak and tired from the beating it has taken these past five months, but his mind remains confident and courageous.

We received fantastic news this week: Collin's latest bone marrow biopsy came back showing zero cancer cells! This means that a bone marrow transplant is no longer necessary. We are so relieved!

Collin is brave, strong, and determined to win this war.

Day 171
June 21, 2021

Today is our 18th wedding anniversary, and we spent it at the cancer clinic. It's not exactly how we imagined celebrating, but our love and commitment to each other is stronger than ever. When we said "yes" to each other 18 years ago, we committed to forever. We were young and head over heels in love. Hand in hand, we were ready to take on the world. Today, we celebrate this special day in a place that is far from the romantic setting I had imagined. But as we sat together in the clinic waiting room, holding hands, and exchanging smiles, I felt so much peace because our love is unbreakable. Together, we tackle each day with courage and determination, finding comfort in each other's presence.

After Collin's medical appointments, we stopped at one of our favorite local restaurants to have an anniversary celebratory lunch. If only for a moment, I desired to escape from the looming presence of cancer, to pretend that it was not sitting at our table. But the reality is we can't outrun it; it follows us wherever we go. Collin, in his valiant effort to make our lunch special, pushed himself, but exhaustion soon caught up with him. We had to cut our outing short, and he spent the rest of the day in bed.

Every day, I remind Collin that his sole job is to focus on healing, and I will handle everything else. And I mean that; I want him to pour every single ounce of energy into himself so he can beat this monster into oblivion, and we can move on with our lives. However, I am left with monumental tasks, and most days, I feel like I am lost in a labyrinth. I stumble, I fall, I break down and cry, and yet I keep putting one foot in front of the other.

While I cannot deny the many blessings and miracles we have experienced, I also have to acknowledge the deep sorrow that accompanies our situation. Most of the time, I try to be strong for Collin and the boys. I focus on gratitude to get me through the hard days. But sometimes, I allow myself to have a pity party. Our situation is my worst nightmare, and today, it feels particularly heavy.

So tonight, I'm struggling through the winding maze of my emotions, feeling lost at every turn. Tomorrow, I'll gather my strength, find the exit, and keep moving forward because I have so much to live for.

Day 177
June 27, 2021

Collin felt strong enough to join us at church today, which was a milestone as it had been months since he could attend. Having him there with us is truly a blessing, as we cherish every moment together. We are grateful for the time we get to spend with him at home. Being in the hospital can be draining, and it's easy to feel consumed by depression, loneliness, and self-pity when confined there.

Day 191
July 11, 2021

The stars aligned, granting Collin and me the chance to escape to Savannah, Georgia, for the weekend. This little getaway was such a gift amidst the chaos that has consumed our lives. I have always dreamed of visiting Savannah, and when we moved to Florida, I was so excited when I discovered it was a short two-hour drive. However, a series of obstacles; COVID-19, the boys' accident, Ian's brain tumor, and Collin's leukemia have thwarted my ability to visit until now. A friend offered to watch our kids, and Collin felt strong enough to travel, so we seized the chance to escape for a few precious days.

Savannah is a walking city, but knowing Collin's limited stamina, we brought along our electric bikes to navigate the charming streets. We had so much fun biking together. It's a simple thing that we used to do together before cancer consumed our lives. In California, we'd

pedal from our home to the beach, and we'd ride along the coastline. After we moved to Florida, we'd bike from our house through lush, tree-lined trails.

We would ride together at least a couple of times a week, and those bike rides were more than just exercise; they were special moments of connection where we shared ideas for our business, discussed our children, and dreamt about our beautiful future together.

These past few days, we immersed ourselves in Savannah's rich history; we indulged in yummy food, and Collin took lots of naps. With Collin's next phase of treatment starting in a few days, this getaway could not have come at a more opportune time. What a blessing this weekend was!

Chapter Four

Intensification Therapy

With induction and consolidation phases behind us, Collin is now transitioning into the third phase of treatment: intensification. In this critical phase, Collin will undergo continued high-dose chemotherapy, targeting any residual leukemia cells that may have evaded previous rounds of treatment.

For Collin, intensification therapy represents another challenging chapter in his brave battle against leukemia. It's a phase that brings uncertainty and challenges, and Collin's body is severely compromised from the months of chemotherapy he has already endured.

But Collin remains hopeful and determined. The objective remains crystal clear: to further diminish the likelihood of relapse and to enhance his long-term prospect for recovery.

Day 216
August 5, 2021

This week, Collin started the intensification phase of treatment. It's supposed to last for a 48-day schedule, but it seems like side effects inevitably arise, often extending each phase an additional thirty days or more. Yesterday, he had a date with the "Red Devil," a chemotherapy drug called doxorubicin, known for its bright red appearance and potential for nasty side effects. Collin has endured seven months of intense chemotherapy, with each treatment becoming progressively more challenging and taking a toll on his recovery. I can't wait for this nightmare to be over. I want my husband back.

Day 231
August 20, 2021

One year ago today, our lives turned upside down, and the memories of that night still haunt me. It was getting late, and I spoke to Ian and Lucah on the phone, just five minutes before everything changed. In an instant, our world shattered, and I shattered right along with it. The boys were in an accident, with Lucah suffering severe injuries that resulted in several surgeries and months of pain. That night, we also discovered Ian had a tumor silently growing in his brain.

While the accident was incredibly traumatic and painful, it turned out to be a blessing in disguise. Out of six passengers, Ian was the only one who had an injury prompting a brain scan. Without the accident, would we have discovered Ian's brain tumor? The neurosurgeon said the accident most likely saved his life.

The accident, Lucah's injuries, Ian's tumor, and Collin's leukemia—these experiences broke me. They didn't just bring me to my knees, they kicked my whole body to the ground. I can't articulate the level of suffering I have experienced this past year. There have been days when I didn't know if I would survive.

I wish I could have told myself then to look for the sun's rays peeking through the storm clouds. When I shifted my focus to gratitude, my mind, body, and spirit began to heal.

I've come to terms with the reality that it's okay not to have it all together, and I've embraced discomfort as a pathway for personal growth. Even amidst life's most challenging moments, I've found glimpses of happiness and reasons to be grateful. Instead of becoming bitter, I became better.

Today, I stand as a different person from who I was a year ago. I've grown in many ways. I am more grounded, humble, gentle, and patient. My heart holds greater compassion, love, and empathy. On the challenging days when the light seems dim, I remind myself that rainbows follow rain, and stars shine brightest in darkness. Courage isn't always loud; sometimes, it's found in the quiet determination to take one step at a time.

Day 240
August 29, 2021

Spending so much time in bed has taken a toll on Collin's strength and muscle mass. To address this, he started in-home physical therapy a few months ago. On Friday, his therapist had him attempt to walk up the stairs in our home. Thank goodness our master bedroom is on the first floor, as he hasn't been strong

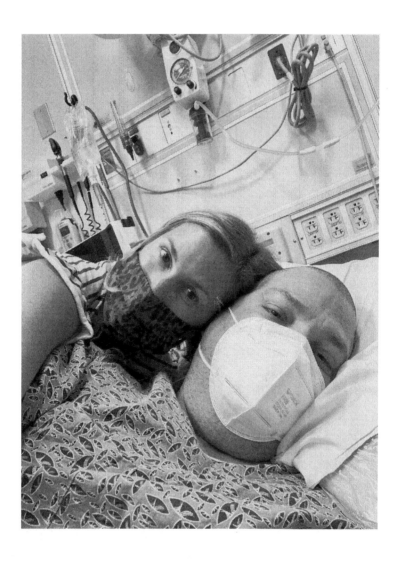

enough to climb stairs for a long time. He successfully made it to the top of the stairs, but he was completely exhausted, which ended their session for the day.

The next day, yesterday, he complained of soreness in his left calf. I worried it may be a blood clot. My mind always jumps to the worst-case scenario. Collin, being his typical self, brushed it off, attributing it to the stairs. Reluctantly, I agreed.

However, this morning, as he was dressing for church, I noticed his left leg had a dusty blue hue. This is an immediate indicator of a blood clot. Of course, neither of us wanted to go to the emergency room, but we knew we needed to get his leg examined. Unfortunately, we discovered he has a massive clot running down his entire leg, and a piece broke off and got stuck in his right lung. We are incredibly lucky to have caught it when we did; the potential outcome could have been far worse.

After a few peaceful months without Collin's hospital admissions, he's back again. Tomorrow they will surgically remove the blood clot in his leg, and he will remain in the hospital for another few days for monitoring. Despite remaining stable and in good spirits, the relentless nature of cancer is undeniable. It's an unforgiving monster.

I snapped this photo in the emergency room before they escorted me out. With COVID cases on the rise, I'm not allowed to accompany him during his hospital admission.

Day 241
August 30, 2021

He's still defying the odds! The procedure to remove the blood clot in Collin's leg went smoothly. They managed to extract the entire clot, which the doctor described as the largest and thickest he'd ever seen! Collin even sent me a picture of it on the surgical table. It was massive, almost resembling a placenta. It was gross! However, it's a testament to the magnitude of what he's been dealing with.

Collin mentioned that his leg already feels much better, and we're optimistic that he'll be able to return home tomorrow afternoon. While they couldn't remove the blood clot in his lung, he's receiving medications to dissolve it. We're feeling incredibly grateful; this situation could have ended in disaster. It's yet another reminder of the many miracles in our lives.

Day 244
September 2, 2021

The following words are Collin's, from his journal:

"I want to share my testimony about angels, both heavenly and earthly, in our lives. After undergoing surgery to remove what my doctor described as the largest and thickest blood clot he had ever seen, I returned to my hospital room for recovery. Because of COVID-19 restrictions, Kelci couldn't be with me, leaving me alone for the first time during a hospital stay.

After waiting for the prescribed four-hour recovery period, I attempted to stand up and use the restroom. To my surprise, the surgical wound on my left leg unexpectedly reopened, causing me to bleed profusely. I'm on extensive blood thinners, so the blood was pouring out from the back of my knee as if from a faucet. In that moment of desperation, I froze. I didn't know what to do. I was thinking, shoot, I'm here all alone. If Kelci was here, she would know what to do. I don't know what to do. I think I'm going to bleed out right here!

Just as I thought that an earthly angel, Nurse Ty, came to my rescue! As I yelled out to her for help, I could see the panic in her eyes. But despite her own fear, she remained calm and quickly went into action to stop the bleeding. I don't know the exact amount of blood I lost today, but the blood soaked completely through the hospital mattress into a puddle on the floor. Without Nurse Ty's intervention, I wouldn't be here today to share this story! I am forever grateful to Ty for saving my life. Today, she was my angel.

Throughout my life, especially during this challenging year, I've encountered many other earthly angels who have ministered to me in various ways. This experience has taught me that we all can be angels to those in need. By listening to promptings and reaching out to serve, we can make a profound difference in someone's life.

I have so much appreciation for everyone who has extended their thoughts and prayers to me and my family. The outpouring of support has been a source of immense comfort during this challenging time. I am deeply grateful for the love and protection I feel from my Heavenly Father and my Savior, Jesus Christ. Their presence is a constant source of reassurance, guiding and comforting me through life's trials. I firmly believe that God has a greater purpose for me, and I place my trust in His divine plan."

Day 266
September 24, 2021

Today marks the final infusion of the intensification phase—the last leg of intense chemotherapy! There were moments when I doubted we'd reach this milestone. It's a monumental victory, but the battle isn't over. On October 18th, Collin will transition to maintenance therapy: daily chemotherapy pills and monthly infusions for 2-3 years.

Cancer's complexity hit us hard. Just 9 months ago, my husband was the epitome of health until he wasn't. Nothing could prepare me for the despair that would come as I helplessly stood by and watched my husband critically deteriorate in front of my eyes. Witnessing Collin's drastic decline, battling not only aggressive leukemia but a host of debilitating side effects has been soul-crushing. It's an indescribable nightmare.

These past 9 months, he has endured- hepatic encephalopathy, liver failure, an enlarged spleen, fevers, mouth sores, blood clots, surgery, intense pain, infections, hair loss, nausea, vomiting, extreme fatigue, weakness, weight loss, weight gain, intense swelling, depression, anxiety, high blood pressure, high cholesterol, blood transfusions, platelet transfusions, neutropenia, anemia, skin rashes, insomnia, mental confusion, memory problems, hyperglycemia, nerve pain, nerve damage, and more. I'm amazed as I watch my husband, who is struggling physically and emotionally, navigate each day with unwavering optimism.

Meanwhile, my list of worries seems endless; the weight of the unknown, the constant "what ifs," leaves me emotionally exhausted, consumed by fear and worry. What surprising side effect will happen next? What if the leukemia gets stronger? What if Ian's brain tumor returns? What is our life going to look like next year? What is our life going to look like in five years?

I keep trying to control the uncontrollable, but the weight and magnitude of our reality easily consume me. Like a rabid beast, it chews me up and spits me back out.

Some people believe that faith protects against the trials of life, but in reality, faith does not function as a shield against pain but serves as a companion to it. So as I continue on this journey of adversity, I hold steadfast to my faith, allowing Jesus Christ to be my source of comfort and support.

This does not take away my pain. It does not make things easy, but it gives me the strength and power to walk through it.

"Come unto me, all ye that labor and are heavy laden, and I will give you rest. Take my yoke upon you and learn of me; for I am meek and lowly in heart: and ye shall find rest unto your souls. For my yoke is easy, and my burden is light." (Matthew 11:28–30)

Chapter Five

Maintenance Therapy

Maintenance therapy signifies the last leg of the marathon, the ultimate push toward the finish line. Unlike the preceding phases, with their intensive treatments, maintenance therapy for Collin entails receiving lower doses of chemotherapy over the next two to three years. Throughout this period, Collin will undergo monthly chemotherapy infusions and adhere to a regimen of daily oral chemotherapy.

Maintenance therapy aims to eradicate any lingering leukemia cells that might persist in the body. We're chasing remission, desperately trying to keep it within our grasp. While the journey is far from over, each step brings us closer to reclaiming the life we once knew, a life untouched by the shadows of leukemia.

Day 290
October 18, 2021

Today marks the first day of the rest of our lives. Collin is officially in maintenance therapy! I honestly wasn't sure if we would ever see this day. Collin never doubted, but I did.

This past year has been emotionally, physically, and spiritually taxing, beyond what I ever imagined possible. I am in survival mode, grappling with the harsh reality of our situation. As a caregiver, I have often felt constrained, unable to express my true feelings genuinely to those around me. I've crafted an unrealistic narrative in my mind, one where I believe I can never share a word of complaint or reveal my humanity. After all, I'm not the one facing cancer, so I convince myself that I have no right to voice my struggles.

So I write in this journal. It's my place to let it all out, to express the heaviness of what we're all going through. Here, I can share the weight of our struggles and find some respite, even if it's momentary, in acknowledging them and putting my feelings into words.

This experience of witnessing my husband's fight for survival has shifted my perspective in profound ways. The caregiver often carries their burden in silence. I transitioned from having a strong, capable partner in life to single-handedly shouldering all the responsibilities of parenting, managing the household, and running our business, all while striving to keep my husband alive. Yet, this silent struggle often goes unseen. Everyone's attention naturally gravitates towards Collin's suffering, and rightfully so. I want him to be the focus of attention, but internally, I'm slowly dying.

If the roles were reversed, I know Collin would do the same for me, and there is nothing I wouldn't do for that man. I am immensely grateful that I am capable of managing all the tasks that need to be done. I am also grateful for my medical knowledge, which has proven invaluable time and time again.

However, I also have to acknowledge the conflicting emotions. Even though it's difficult for me to admit, sometimes, I find myself feeling resentful and angry at Collin for being sick. I resent the fact that I am effectively a solo mom to four boys with a husband who is chronically ill. I am angry that my life is no longer my own, and cancer controls it.

I know how awful this makes me sound, and I am so ashamed I have these thoughts and feelings. But I miss our old life. I miss having a partner, being carefree, and going on extravagant family vacations or impromptu adventures. I miss the simple joy of going to the beach whenever we felt like it and being playful and spontaneous with my kids. Sometimes I look in the mirror and feel like I'm just a shell of my former self. I don't recognize who I am anymore. I'm exhausted, and I've lost myself in this diagnosis. My every thought, my every action, revolves around cancer. If it doesn't have to do with life or death, it doesn't earn my attention.

I've gone to extreme lengths to keep our children's lives as unaffected as possible. I've worked tirelessly to keep our business up and running and consistently put everyone else's needs above my own. However, the truth is, beneath the surface, a simmering resentment has begun to take root. As guilty as these thoughts make me feel, I can't pretend they aren't here. Of course, I would never express this to Collin. But he knows me better than anyone, and I'm certain he is aware of my feelings.

I have such high hopes for this next phase. While Collin will still receive chemotherapy, it won't be at the same intensity. So, I'm hopeful to get him back to at least 50% capacity. I miss him, I miss the person I am when I'm with him, and I miss us. Just two people, carefree and passionately in love. My soul aches to get us back.

Day 305
November 2, 2021

Today I peeked into Collin's journal. Don't worry, I wasn't snooping. He knows I read it from time to time. This is what he wrote:

"Life presents us with two options: things either happen to us or they happen for us. It's all about perspective. That doesn't mean life is always sunshine and rainbows, but it means that we can accept, confront, overcome, and learn from every challenge.

Over the past year, I have strived to maintain a perspective of gratitude, even when it felt impossible. My mind, body, and spirit have been bruised and broken. However, I am incredibly grateful to share that my latest bone marrow biopsy reveals zero leukemia cells! Though I still have a long way to go before life returns to normal, I am committed to never giving up and I will emerge from this war stronger and better than ever."

Gosh, I love this man. He is far from perfect, but he is perfect for me!

Day 334
December 1, 2021

I'm brimming with high hopes for the approaching holidays, eagerly expecting the chance to make them as special as possible for Collin and the boys. It has always been our family's favorite time of year, and typically, Collin and I go all out to make the festivities extra special for everyone. Given his reduced stamina this year, I insisted he rest while I took charge of creating all the Christmas magic.

Truth be told, I need this holiday season. For me, it symbolizes a future filled with hope, a sign that our lives are slowly but surely returning to a semblance of normalcy. Last week, I spent hours and hours every day decking out our home with Christmas decor. Both the inside and outside of our house look like Christmas exploded on it, and I love it!

Collin's physical energy has been steadily improving with each passing day. Though he may not have fully regained his previous capacity, which I recognize may take time, I would estimate his current strength to be around 40% to 50% of what it was a year ago.

He caught a viral cold during the week of Thanksgiving. The cough is still lingering, but his doctor has reassured us that there's no cause for concern, and we don't need to worry about it too much.

Day 350
December 17, 2021

I'm slowly witnessing the return of my husband! Don't get me wrong; he still has a long road ahead, but I am starting to see a glimmer of light at the end of this very long tunnel. For the first time all year, I feel like we are gradually regaining control of our lives. While cancer is still riding shotgun, it is no longer in the driver's seat, and that feels so amazing!

Tonight, we attended a Christmas party hosted by our friends. Collin only lasted about an hour before fatigue set in, prompting us to leave early. But the simple fact that he felt well enough to even try to attend is an enormous sign of progress.

As for the lingering cough and congestion Collin experienced after catching a cold during Thanksgiving week, it appears to have progressed into an ear infection. He is currently receiving treatment with oral antibiotics and antibiotic ear drops. I am a little nervous about it since his immune system is still compromised after months of intense chemotherapy. Hopefully, it will clear up soon.

Day 364
December 31, 2021

I am more than ready to say goodbye to 2021. As I reflect on what has been the hardest year of my life, I cannot deny that amidst the struggles, I've also witnessed countless miracles and blessings.

This year tested our resilience, pushing our family to its limits. Yet, amidst the challenges, we discovered an inner strength and an unwavering resolve to persevere. Even in the chaos, there were moments of pure magic. We witnessed many acts of kindness and compassion that restored our faith in humanity. We celebrated both small victories and major triumphs. And through it all, our family grew individually and collectively in ways we never thought possible.

I'm eager to enter a new year and leave 2021 behind. However, I do so with a mixture of trepidation and excitement. I know life will not always be easy, but if there is one thing 2021 taught me, it is that every trial and hardship is an opportunity for miracles and blessings.

Chapter Six

Relapse

Relapse in leukemia occurs when residual cancer cells survive despite treatment and subsequently become resistant to further therapy. It's a distressing scenario, as these resistant cells can proliferate, leading to a resurgence of the disease. Managing relapsed leukemia poses significant challenges compared to treating newly diagnosed cases, primarily because of the gained resistance to previous treatments.

The resilience of leukemia cells against conventional therapies complicates the treatment approach, often requiring more aggressive interventions to combat the resistant cancer cells effectively.

The statistics surrounding relapsed leukemia, especially for adults with acute lymphoblastic leukemia like Collin, paint a sobering picture. Only approximately 10% of patients with relapsed leukemia are alive five years later.

For Collin, the possibility of leukemia relapse looms as a daunting reality, casting a shadow of uncertainty over our lives. Despite enduring rounds of intensive chemotherapy and facing each day with unwavering determination, there's a persistent fear that some leukemia cells may have evaded treatment, lurking within his body and potentially resistant to further interventions.

Day 367
January 3, 2022

We wanted to kick off this new year with something special, so today we hopped aboard a cruise ship! Collin and I were eager for some family fun and quality time together. We've missed our adventures, so for Christmas, we surprised the boys with a cruise vacation to the Western Caribbean for five nights of sun, sea, and relaxation.

Given Collin's limited stamina, a cruise seemed like the perfect getaway. The boys can enjoy the ship's activities while Collin and I take it easy, adjusting our plans based on how he's feeling. While I'm excited about this much-needed break, I can't shake off my nerves about being far from home and Collin's medical team.

The oncology team gave us clearance to travel after Collin's recent blood work, despite some elevated inflammation markers. Though I expressed my concerns, they reassured us that they were not worried and encouraged us to enjoy our vacation.

Because of pandemic protocols, every passenger is required to undergo COVID-19 testing before boarding the ship. The line was super long, and poor Collin had to stand for two hours straight. By the time we got onboard this ship, he was utterly exhausted.

We are now setting sail. I am sitting outside on the balcony as I write this, Collin is napping. The water glistens in the sunlight, a million shimmering lights dancing on the waves. A mix of excitement and apprehension stirs within me. I hope this trip will bring the relaxation and joy we all so desperately need. Here's to cherishing every moment together, despite the uncertainties that lie ahead.

Day 368
January 4, 2022

Today has been quite challenging. Collin isn't feeling his best. All day, he's been struggling with a significant backache, which, coupled with general fatigue, has left him worn out. He is keeping food down, but he doesn't have an appetite. For most of the day, he laid in bed while I did a few things around the ship with the boys. After dinner, we were looking forward to catching a comedy show, but he just wasn't up for it.

I'm worried. Collin thinks it's just because he overdid it yesterday, standing in line, but my intuition is telling me something else. I'm trying to stay positive, but it's tough. It's easy for my mind to go to the worst-case scenarios.

I'm hoping tomorrow brings a better day for him. We will be in Cozumel, Mexico. I'm keeping a close eye on him, and we'll take things one step at a time.

Day 369
January 5, 2022

Despite Collin's assurances that he's okay, worry kept me tossing and turning all night. And today, here in Cozumel, Mexico, my fears reached a terrifying reality.

I was prepared to take the boys off the ship by myself, but Collin insisted on coming along despite not feeling well. We had planned to go snorkeling, but the weather was a little stormy, making the ocean visibility murky. The boys and Collin decided they wanted to explore the jungle on ATVs, guided by a local expert who also promised to show us a stunning cenote.

We jumped on ATVs, and I could see Collin struggling, trying his best to keep up for the sake of the boys and me. It's heartbreaking to witness him struggle with tasks that used to be second nature to him. All he wants is to feel "normal" again.

On our way back to the ship, things took a turn for the worse. Collin grew pale, mentioning a sudden pain in his right upper abdomen. When I felt his forehead, it was burning up; I didn't have a thermometer, but I could tell he had a fever. My heart sank as I realized this was not from standing in the COVID testing line two days ago.

His symptoms suggest that he could have gallstones, a potential side effect of his chemotherapy.

My mind is racing with worry. There is a doctor onboard, but what could the ship's medical clinic possibly do for him? I remembered our previous experience a few years ago, when Maddox had an accident on a cruise ship. He slipped on the stairs going up to the water-slide and sliced open his eyebrow. The ship's medical clinic, although sufficient for minor things, has limited resources, and they would likely just send Collin to a hospital in Mexico.

The mere thought of navigating a foreign healthcare system amidst Collin's complicated medical history sends shivers down my spine. Collin cannot afford to be stranded in a Mexican hospital; that much is certain.

I'm panicking, clinging to prayer as my only lifeline. Right now, it feels like my only option is to get Collin back to the United States for proper medical care. This uncertainty is overwhelming, but I'll do whatever it takes to ensure Collin gets the help he needs. I have no choice but to believe I will figure this out.

Day 370
January 6, 2022

This is the cruise from hell and it can't end soon enough. All I want is to disembark from this ship and get home. Last night, I tried our best to keep Collin as comfortable as possible by using cold rags and arranging blankets and pillows around him. The pain is getting more intense and is wrapping around from the middle of his abdomen to his upper back. I believe he has gallstones.

Terrifying nightmares plagued me the few times I closed my eyes for sleep. I kept envisioning Collin being medically evacuated from the ship by helicopter, but in my nightmare, I couldn't go with him because someone needed to stay on board with the boys. It was utterly horrific, imagining Collin alone in some strange hospital where he doesn't speak the language, the doctors not knowing his medical history, and me clueless about how to find him.

Today, we're docked in the Bahamas on the cruise line's private island, but the Bahamian government isn't allowing anyone to leave the ship, likely because of COVID-19 concerns. However, even if we could disembark, I wouldn't feel comfortable leaving Collin alone on the ship.

I'm trying my best to maintain a cheerful facade for the boys and Collin. I don't want the boys to worry, and I know Collin already feels like he's ruined this vacation, which tears me up inside.

He's been able to keep fluids down, and I'm doing everything I can to keep him hydrated. But the nagging fear persists—if he becomes dehydrated, I'll have no choice but to take him to the ship's medical clinic. That dreaded scenario looms in my mind: a medical evacuation.

I'm trying hard not to blame myself. But why did I think a cruise was a good idea? All I wanted was a few days of normalcy. But now I realize this was way too soon. I'm filled with so much guilt and regret.

Day 371
January 7, 2022

Today we are at sea, and it is the last day of this hellish cruise. Tomorrow can't come soon enough! I've already spoken to the guest services staff, letting them know we'll be self-carrying our luggage and eager to disembark as soon as possible, which they said will probably be around 7:00 am. Of course, I didn't divulge the reason behind our urgency; I've remained tight-lipped about Collin's condition, fearing the possibility of my nightmares of him being medically evacuated becoming a reality.

Collin's symptoms still align with a potential gallstone diagnosis, but naturally, I can't shake the worry that this could be a recurrence of leukemia. I've asked Collin multiple times if he suspects it's leukemia, and if he's concerned that the cancer has returned. Each time, he reassures me that this pain feels different from the leukemia pain he had before. He firmly believes it's related to his gallbladder. His words offer a sliver of comfort, but my worry persists.

Day 372
January 8, 2022

6:55 am: Collin has been vomiting all morning. It's clear that he's not strong enough to walk off the ship. I phoned the ship's medical clinic, urgently requesting a wheelchair and explaining our medical emergency, emphasizing our need for priority disembarkation. They suggested we see the ship's doctor before leaving, but I declined, knowing it would only delay our departure.

8:00 am: We've made it off the ship and onto solid ground in the United States! Thankfully, customs was a breeze, and we quickly reached our parked car. I called Collin's medical team, providing them with a detailed update. They agreed it sounded like gallstones and instructed us to head straight to the hospital, where they would alert the emergency room staff of our pending arrival.

12:35 pm: The surrealism of this situation is overwhelming. Exactly one year ago today, Collin received his leukemia diagnosis, with a mere 30% chance of survival past the first year. Now, 365 days later, we find ourselves back at the same hospital.

Currently, we are in the emergency room, waiting for the results of Collin's abdominal CT scan and ultrasound to confirm gallstones. I had high hopes for 2022. I believed, foolishly, that the change in the calendar year was going to magically make things better. I long for the simplicity of normalcy, where mundane tasks like laundry and dinner plans are my biggest daily stressors. Unfortunately, we are only eight days into the year and every single day has been a battle. But I have to believe that better days are coming.

2:05 pm: I am traumatized and terrified. Growing impatient waiting for the doctor to give us results and answers, I logged into Collin's patient portal and found the radiology report from the CT scan. With trembling hands, I read it; the results are devastating. Collin's pain is not from gallstones. His gallbladder appears fine. There are lesions on his liver, suggesting the leukemia has returned. Though we haven't received official confirmation from the doctor, I have read the report repeatedly to ensure I understood the radiologist's findings correctly. Unfortunately, I did.

I didn't want to alarm Collin until the doctor confirmed this. But I can't hide my emotions from him; he can read me like a book. As Collin slept, I paced the room, consumed by fear. When he woke, (I still hadn't told him I saw the report stating he had lesions on his liver) he saw me pacing the floor and said, "Babe, it's going to be okay. I'll be fine."

Through tears, I asked how he could be so sure. Sensing I knew more, he confided, "Kelci, I know." Confused, I replied, "You know what?" He said, "The Spirit told me two days ago that the leukemia has returned. I didn't tell you because I didn't want you to worry."

I immediately started sobbing and dropped to my knees on the floor. Why is this happening? I don't understand why God would allow this to happen to us. Haven't we suffered enough? Haven't we already learned all that we were supposed to learn from this horrid experience? What more does He expect from us? I have nothing more to give. I am completely depleted, deflated, and feel swallowed by defeat.

The hematologists have warned us: if leukemia returns after remission, it's nearly impossible to eradicate. I'm at a loss for words. I am crushed.

Day 375
January 11, 2022

The hospital admitted Collin because the leukemia is angry and aggressive. It's come back with a vengeance. Collin is in agonizing pain, the narcotics that he is getting through his IV are barely taking the edge off. The aggressive nature of this recurrent leukemia is evident in Collin's deteriorating condition.

The doctors delivered a somber prognosis, explaining that the chemotherapy that we used to fight off the leukemia before most likely will not be effective in this battle. Instead, they've turned to immunotherapies as our new hope for treatment. Today he started the immunotherapy drug Blincyto. The doctors have set very realistic expectations, telling us there is no guarantee it is going to work and it may cause life-threatening side effects, but we are running out of options, so we must try. The hope is that the Blincyto will kill the leukemia and bring Collin's leukemic count down low enough that he will be eligible for a bone marrow transplant. Since the leukemia has returned, a transplant is now Collin's only hope for survival.

This new reality has sent me into a tailspin. I am not okay; the weight of this burden is too much to carry. Witnessing Collin's rapid decline has brought me a new overwhelming sense of helplessness and despair. As

Collin embarks on his first round of immunotherapy today, I am experiencing a torrent of emotions. I am so scared.

Despite the daunting road ahead, Collin's unwavering resolve and faith serve as fuel that I am using to keep going. I must hold on to my belief and search for the light. It's the only way forward, the only way to navigate through this darkness. So I'll press on, clinging to the possibility that a brighter tomorrow is indeed within our grasp. As I have experienced countless times, even on the darkest days, glimmers of light can be found.

Day 376
January 12, 2022

We're witnessing another miracle — the new drug Blincyto is working! Collin's white blood cell count and leukemic cell count are both decreasing, marking significant progress. His pain has improved immensely, which is an incredible relief. Today, he achieved a major milestone: getting out of bed and sitting in a chair, which is absolutely huge! This has really boosted his spirits. He's ready to keep fighting with everything he's got.

The doctors are encouraged, but they emphasized the need to strike a balanced pace in treating the leukemia, to avoid what's known as tumor lysis syndrome. This syndrome occurs when leukemic cells die and release substances into the blood. These substances can lead to various life-threatening complications. My mind is in overdrive, trying to keep up with the complexities of everything. Everyone keeps telling me to lean on my support system, but Collin is my support system. He is the one I need; he is the one I want to lean on, and I can't.

Leaving Collin every night is one of the toughest things I have to do. Coming home without him feels surreal, like I'm living someone else's life, because there's no way this is my reality. It's a struggle to go to bed without him; our bed feels so empty. Maddox and Elijah have started taking turns sleeping in my bed with me. It's become a routine now, comforting for all of us. But deep down, it's Collin I miss the most.

I'm grateful he's still here fighting, but it's just not the same. How could it be? It hurts so much to see him struggling. I just want him back the way he was. I miss us. I feel like a piece of me has gone missing. I have lost myself in this process, in trying to keep him alive. I am grateful that I can do this, but I also hate it all at the same time. It's this strange duality I live with every day. On one hand, I cherish every moment he's still here, every breath he takes a precious gift. On the other hand, the relentless battle is eroding my spirit. I'm caught between gratitude and exhaustion, between hope and despair. It's tearing me apart, piece by piece, yet I can't imagine doing anything else.

Every day is a battle. This is torturous. There is nothing more I want than him to be well, to have this nightmare behind us, and to have things go back to normal, the way they used to be.

Yet, I realize that even if Collin does indeed beat this, our life will never be quite the same. The scars and battle wounds of this journey will linger, reshaping our reality in ways we can't yet foresee. Until then, I'll keep holding onto hope and cherishing every moment we have together.

Day 377
January 13, 2022

Collin shared a special experience with me this morning. But first, let me back up three days ago to give some context. One of my dearest friends, Jessica, brought me lunch at the hospital. Collin was in extreme pain, and despite receiving all the pain medication he could safely have, his pain level remained at a ten out of ten. Jessica and I joined forces to help him relax, standing quietly by his bedside—me at his head and she at his feet. We didn't speak a word to avoid disturbing him, but we both gently stroked his skin, to calm him and hopefully provide some pain relief.

This morning, Collin recounted that experience and said, "Kelci, I knew you and Jessica both had your hands on me, but I also felt dozens of other hands on my body. I heard voices of so many other women, voices that I didn't recognize, and some were in other languages. Even though I was in excruciating pain, I felt so much comfort. I felt love and peace. I know that there were others we could not see in the room with us. Not only could I feel them, but I could hear them."

One might hear that and think that Collin is going crazy. Say he is hallucinating, but I believe him 100%. We have thousands of people around the world praying for us right now, and we can feel the power of those supportive prayers. There have been many moments these past few days when I felt like I just didn't have it in me to keep going. In those moments, I felt like I was surrounded by angels, giving me the support I needed to continue.

I know we are not alone in this battle. There are forces from both sides of heaven working in our favor. I know Collin isn't just fighting for himself, or me and our sons, but he is also fighting for them as well.

Day 381
January 17, 2022

Collin urgently needs additional prayers. We need another miracle. Two days ago, Collin began to feel agonizing pain again in his lower chest and upper abdomen. He was making so much progress, and the pain came back out of nowhere. The doctors have done extensive testing and cannot pinpoint the source of his suffering. I questioned the oncology team if leukemia could cause this pain, but they said leukemia typically isn't this painful.

This has led us to suspect that the Blincyto he started last week may be causing these harmful side effects. As a result, all chemotherapy and immunotherapy have been stopped to allow his body time to recover.

This is super scary because this pause will allow the leukemia to gain momentum and strength. His leukemic cell count has been steadily decreasing every day since we started the immunotherapy, but in the last two days, it has plateaued at 35%. I am so nervous it will begin to increase again.

In addition to the pain, Collin is also battling a significant buildup of fluid in his lungs, which is making it harder for him to breathe on his own. He is now on BiPAP, and I pray that will be sufficient and he will not need to go on a ventilator. Each day feels like an uphill climb. We conquer one mountain only to be confronted by another, and then another. I am utterly drained.

Day 383
January 19, 2022

This week has been the hardest thus far. Collin is going downhill fast; leukemia has hijacked his body. Today, the doctors delivered devastating news. His leukemic cell count has skyrocketed to 90%. His body is falling apart, different body systems are failing: his liver, kidneys, and lungs, each organ struggling under the weight of this merciless disease.

During morning rounds, the fear in the doctors' eyes was palpable. One by one, specialists entered, but not one could offer us much hope. I'm gripped by panic and devastation, unsure of what to do next. The thought of losing Collin is unbearable.

As his condition worsens, I'm faced with the agonizing decision of how much to share with our boys. I've tried to shield them from the severity of Collin's illness, but one of my worst fears is Collin dying and me not giving our children the chance to say their goodbyes.

The boys are currently at school, but I think I need to call someone to bring them to the hospital. Ugh, this is freaking impossible! I wish I could ask Collin what to do, but he is barely coherent, and he is in so much pain, he wouldn't even be able to think clearly.

I hate everything about this! I want to yell and scream, but I am too broken to muster even the slightest energy to do so. The weight of this is crushing me. I have nothing left. I am utterly depleted. Every ounce of strength has been drained from my soul; there are no words to articulate the depth of my despair. I'm begging and pleading for heaven's help.

Day 384
January 20, 2022

Watching the people you love suffer with no power to do anything to relieve that suffering is the definition of hell. I am currently sitting in hell.

Yesterday, I had our friend pull the boys out of school and bring them to the hospital. I tried to prepare them for what they would see: Collin hooked to machines, barely coherent. But nothing could truly prepare them for the reality of the situation.

The look in their eyes screamed terror, and they looked at me for reassurance, for safety. I'm trying my best, but how can I provide safety in a place filled with so much uncertainty and fear?

As excruciatingly painful as this is, I think I did the right thing by bringing them to the hospital. Our sons got to spend precious moments with their dad. He held their hands; he mustered the strength to open his eyes and speak a few words to each of them. I could see how much he cherished having them there, but I also saw the trauma this experience inflicted on them.

This is not fair! A child should never have to face the distress of wondering if it's the last time they'll see their dad alive. Why must our family endure this agony?

Last night, after the boys went home, I had a sobering conversation with the oncology team. They stopped all cancer treatments 3 days ago because Collin is medically unstable from the side effects of the immunotherapy. But during our conversation last night, the hematologist emphasized the urgent need to continue with therapy anyway. She told me if we don't do something to tame the leukemia, Collin will die very soon.

The medical team got insurance approval to initiate a new treatment regimen. This protocol involves a combination of chemotherapy and an immunotherapy drug called Besponsa. It's a last-ditch effort, and there is a lot of uncertainty and no guarantees. The oncologist admitted that this treatment might kill him. But if we do nothing, the leukemia is certain to kill him.

Collin received his first dose of Besponsa last night, and now we wait, holding onto hope and praying for another miracle. This morning, his leukemic cell count was holding steady at 90%. I know God is capable, and our faith remains steadfast. Despite the uncertainty, I'm trying to drop my resistance, meaning I am trying to accept whatever is God's will, however difficult it may be.

Day 386
January 22, 2022

The Besponsa appears to be working! Yesterday, Collin's leukemia count dropped to 74% and today, it dropped even more to 43%. This is huge! His liver and kidney function numbers are stabilizing, as well as his lung function, marking further improvement in his condition. I can't express how grateful I am that he is finally improving and heading in the right direction. This is a miracle! Only three days ago, I was preparing to say goodbye to him, and now, if he continues to improve, he will eventually be able to come home!

In moments of overwhelming troubles, worries, or sorrows, I remind myself to seek the light. I have to make a conscious effort to do this because I am surrounded by darkness, and the light seems so elusive. I know the light is there, it's just waiting to be found. Once discovered, I hold on to it tightly, drawing courage from its glow, and I push forward. I understand that dwelling in darkness only leads to further despair. It's the light that is giving me the strength to persevere.

Day 389
January 25, 2022

God continues to answer our prayers. This morning, his leukemic cell count was down to 12%. Hallelujah! Collin is getting stronger every single day. If he continues progressing, he will come home in a few days!

Day 393
January 29, 2022

After enduring three grueling weeks in the hospital, losing over 50 pounds, and enduring unbearable physical pain, Collin has finally returned home! While this hospital stay wasn't the longest we've experienced, it was undoubtedly the hardest. As his vital organs began to fail, he fought with every ounce of strength to cling to life. On one of the darkest days, he asked me between labored breaths, if he was dying. Indeed, he was, and at that moment, I was terrified and couldn't help but wonder how much longer his battered body could endure the relentless battle. Yet, once again, God has graced us with another miracle!

We don't know what God has in store for us. But as we navigate these most frightful days, I am committed to making the most of each moment and to trying my best to learn from these experiences. This world was never designed to be fair, but we know God has a plan. We will continue to put our trust in Him, albeit difficult at times.

Day 401
February 6, 2022

We're just soaking up every single moment of having Collin back home. It's been tough, no doubt about it. Yet, seeing him here seems almost surreal. Even though he's not feeling great, it's like a weight has been lifted off my shoulders. I am just so happy he's still here with us.

Collin is getting a little stronger every day. It's slow progress, but it's progress. He remains profoundly weak and tired and is reliant on around-the-clock narcotics to manage his pain. It's truly agonizing for me to witness him in this condition. Despite everything, Collin is still smiling. He's got this amazing resilience about him that just shines through, even on the toughest days.

Maddox was so excited because Collin could make it to his flag football game yesterday. Collin has missed out on so much with our sons, and he was determined not to miss this opportunity to support Maddox. As we arrived at the field, I was nervous. I wasn't sure if Collin could walk the distance from the parked car to the game field. But he surprised me, per usual! Despite his fatigue, his eyes lit up with enthusiasm as he watched Maddox take the field.

As I witnessed this moment, I couldn't help but feel a sense of gratitude wash over me. Our family is so blessed with an abundance of love that binds us together.

Right now, we are just taking one day at a time, cherishing these moments we have together. Because the thing that gets us through is love, and no matter how tough things get, no matter what happens, our love will never end.

Day 403
February 9, 2022

We had the privilege of meeting with the Bone Marrow Transplant Team at Southeastern Memorial today. We feel immensely grateful for the opportunity to access treatment from two of the nation's foremost cancer treatment centers, starting with Jackson Miller and now continuing with Southeastern Memorial Hospital. While Collin continues to receive treatments at Jackson Miller Medical Institute, Southeastern Memorial is diligently preparing for the next crucial phase: the bone marrow transplant.

Four different hematology oncologists have confirmed that since the leukemia has returned, Collin's only chance for survival is a successful bone marrow transplant. The transplant process is very intense and potentially fatal, but we are confident in the plan. Currently, all four of his siblings are being tested to see if they qualify as a donor. We are praying one of his siblings is a match, since this provides the best chance of success.

Next week, Collin will get a bone marrow biopsy and then he will return to the hospital for more inpatient therapy. If the stars align, Collin should be ready for transplant to take place at the end of March, or early April.

Most days on this journey feel like too much to handle. Yet, amidst the turmoil, I hold on to the belief that every day is a precious gift. Good days bring joy and happiness, reminding me of life's blessings. The bad days teach me things and help me grow.

Even in the darkest moments, I find strength and learn valuable lessons. And when the sun shines its brightest, those are the days I treasure most.

Day 406
February 11, 2022

Remember the ear infection Collin had back in December? The one triggered by the viral cold he caught right before Thanksgiving. Well, apparently that stubborn infection hasn't budged an inch since then.

During Collin's last hospital stay, amidst the excruciating pain of leukemia wreaking havoc on his body, he kept complaining about his left ear, the very one infected back in December. I brought it up with both the oncology and infectious disease doctors several times. Their response was consistent: the potent IV antibiotics he was receiving should have annihilated any lingering infection in his middle ear. They likened it to using a bazooka against a fly, and I agreed. After all, our focus was on combating much larger adversaries than a measly ear infection.

Yet, it seems the bazooka wasn't quite up to the task, as the stubborn ear infection persists. This morning, Collin mentioned his left ear was aching, and he was experiencing a noticeable decrease in his hearing. I knew this wasn't good, so I sprang into action, dialing every ear, nose, and throat specialist (ENT) in the area, desperate for an immediate appointment. Most offices, frustratingly, couldn't accommodate us until a month out. Waiting isn't an option. Collin and I both hate going to the emergency room, but I made it clear to him that if we couldn't find an available appointment, I would have to take him.

Miraculously, I found an ENT with an appointment for today. Without hesitation, I seized the opportunity. Rushing Collin to the appointment, the doctor shared our surprise at the persistence of this ear infection. He elaborated on how lingering infections can cause the fluid behind the ear to congeal, resembling thick, adhesive glue, rendering antibiotics ineffective until the fluid is drained. The doctor revealed that Collin would require surgical placement of ear tubes to facilitate the drainage process. The bad news kept coming. It's not just the middle ear that's affected, the infection has spread to his outer ear, causing significant swelling of his ear canal. No wonder Collin has been having trouble hearing out of that ear!

The doctor prescribed additional antibiotics and ear drops to manage the infection and hopefully decrease some of the swelling in his outer ear before the scheduled surgery. Feeling disheartened, we left the office, trying to accept the reality of yet another medical procedure looming over us. But it has to be done. Collin is scheduled for the ear tube insertion next week on Friday, and then he can get rid of this ear infection for good!

Day 408
February 13, 2022

My friend Brandy reached out to me a few days ago and offered to take photos of our family in our home. She is such a sweet friend and an amazing photographer, so of course I eagerly accepted her offer. Today was the day we had scheduled for the photo shoot. It was

quite a challenge to get everyone to cooperate. Elijah complained about the clothes I picked for him to wear; Collin expressed feeling self-conscious about his appearance and weight gain; Ian and Lucah argued about something insignificant; and Maddox focused more on playing with toys than getting ready for pictures.

In my efforts to keep everyone happy, I felt very stressed. When Brandy knocked on the door, four of us were in tears. We pulled ourselves together and made it through the photo shoot. Brandy already sent me a few sneak peek pictures, and I can't express how grateful I am for these beautiful photos.

Despite the weight of uncertainty and fear that is ever present in our lives, Brandy's thoughtful gesture brought a glimmer of joy and hope. In each frame, I see not just smiles frozen in time, but I also see unconditional love and profound resilience. These photos are more than just images; they are reminders of the never-ending love that binds us together, the laughter that echoes through our home despite the hardships, and the unwavering support of friends like Brandy.

Day 409
February 14, 2022

Today marks yet another Valentine's Day spent in medical offices. It's surreal to realize this has been our reality for over a year now. In some ways, it's hard to remember what life was like before all this. But in other ways, it seems like just yesterday we were immersed in the routines of a typical family.

I vividly recall those mornings. They often began with the gentle sound of the alarm clock, followed by the sleepy shuffling of feet as we all stumbled out of bed. There was laughter and chaos as one kid couldn't find their shoes and another argued about who stole their water bottle.

After breakfast, I would drop the boys off at school, and Collin would dive into a flurry of emails and phone calls, striving to balance work with the demands of family life. By midmorning, we would reconvene for a quick workout together or a spontaneous midday lunch date.

The afternoons were a whirlwind of activity. There were sports practices to attend, playdates to organize, errands to run, and occasionally impromptu dance parties in the living room. We were always on the move, always with a hundred things on our minds.

But amidst the chaos, there were moments of tranquility. Moments spent curled up together on the couch or taking leisurely evening walks as the sun dipped below the horizon. It was those simple, ordinary moments that I miss the most. I can't help but long for those days of normalcy.

Day 411
February 16, 2022

We've received Collin's biopsy results! His bone marrow has 1.5% leukemia cells, and while it's not zero like we were hoping for, it's pretty darn close! Collin will be readmitted to the hospital next week for more inpatient immunotherapy in the hopes that we can keep the leukemia under control. His leukemic cell count must be below 5% to proceed with a bone marrow transplant.

In the meantime, the search for a match continues. We pray he has a sibling match, because this will be the easiest route, but it takes a while to process their blood tests. We should find out in another one and a half to two weeks if any of his four siblings match with him. If the siblings don't match, then they will search the national donor registry for potential donors.

Having Collin home over the past week and a half has been a blessing beyond measure. There's a profound sense of peace when he's with us, and our family is together under one roof. This simple thing that so many take for granted brings a warmth and comfort to my soul that is indescribable.

Day 413
February 18, 2022

Today was supposed to be the day for Collin's ear tube surgery. However, things didn't pan out like we expected. The infection and swelling in Collin's outer ear have worsened, leading to the complete closure of his ear canal. The ENT doctor expressed concerns that the infection might have spread to the bone behind his ear, a condition known as mastoiditis. He ordered an emergency CT scan, which confirmed this fear.

Once we discovered this, the ENT doctor called Collin's infectious disease doctor (thankfully, she gave me her personal cell phone number), and they both agreed that Collin needed to be admitted to the hospital immediately. Of course, Collin is not happy about being in the hospital again, but mastoiditis demands six weeks of intense intravenous (IV) antibiotic treatment, along with surgery to remove the infected portion of the bone and to drain the infected fluid stuck in his middle ear.

The root of this ordeal lies in Collin's compromised immune system, a consequence of his ongoing chemotherapy and immunotherapy treatments. It's a cruel irony, the very treatments meant to save his life seem intent on destroying his remaining health. Collin has been through hell and back with these treatments, and it feels like every time he takes one step forward, he gets knocked two steps back.

It's like a frustrating game of whack-a-mole. Just as we gain ground on one front, another battle emerges. This infection not only inflicts physical pain on Collin, but until he finishes the six-week course of IV antibiotics, he cannot receive any more chemotherapy or immunotherapy. He was supposed to get more infusions of Besponza next week, and without those treatments, his leukemia cell count is almost certain to increase again.

This situation is heavy, and it's dire. I'm trying not to freak out, but I'm freaking out!

Chapter Seven

Mastoidectomy

A mastoidectomy is a surgical procedure used to remove infected or damaged tissue from the mastoid bone, which is located behind the ear. This bone is part of the skull and can become infected in conditions such as mastoiditis, where bacteria spread from the middle ear to the mastoid bone. During a mastoidectomy, the surgeon removes the infected portion of the mastoid bone to treat the infection and prevent it from spreading further.

The mastoid bone is located very close to the brain, and if the infection is left untreated or becomes aggressive, it can extend into the surrounding tissues, including the brain. This can lead to serious complications such as meningitis, brain abscess, other neurological problems, and even death.

Time is of the essence, and it's currently not on Collin's side. With recurrent leukemia living in his bone marrow, every tick of the clock is precious. Collin's immune system is already compromised by the infection and leukemia. Administering chemotherapy or immunotherapy will further suppress his immune system, exacerbate Collin's condition, and increase the risk of complications. It's essential to prioritize treating the mastoiditis and stabilize Collin's condition before resuming chemotherapy. Once the infection is under control and Collin's immune system has recovered sufficiently, his leukemia treatments can resume.

Day 414
February 19, 2022

This morning, the ENT on call for the weekend at the hospital, came in to examine Collin and discuss his mastoidectomy surgery. With a serious expression, he said, "Mr. Jager, I want to be upfront with you. I'm confident in my skills, but looking at your CT scan, I can see the infection is severe and dangerously close to the brain. I'm not comfortable proceeding with this surgery."

My heart sank, and I felt a rush of heat come up from my belly and wash over my face. I recognize this feeling, it's fear and doubt. You would think by now I would be used to these blindsides, but I'm not. This sudden blow came with emotions I wasn't expecting to experience today. I should know by now to always expect the unexpected. To prepare for the worst and hope for the best. When the doctor said he wasn't comfortable proceeding, I felt the ground slipping away beneath me, for what seemed like the millionth time.

But he continued, offering a glimmer of hope. "There's a specialist, Dr. Emerson, who excels in complex surgeries like this. I'll reach out to him, and we'll get you taken care of ASAP. You should expect him to come see you on Monday."

In the midst of uncertainty and fear, Collin remains typically steadfast and faithful. He reminded me to be grateful for the doctor's honesty and determination to find the best possible care for him. Although Collin admits he is nervous, he is also confident that all will be well in the end.

I wish I could share Collin's optimism, but I'm wrestling with a storm of conflicting emotions—hope and doubt, faith and fear. Truthfully, panic is winning. Yet, I have no choice but to hang tight until Monday, when we see Dr. Emerson.

Day 416
February 21, 2022

I can't even wrap my head around what's happening right now. Today was supposed to be the day Dr. Emerson came in to meet Collin and get his surgery scheduled. But instead, we got a different ENT; not the one we saw on Saturday, not Dr. Emerson, a whole unfamiliar face.

And then, the bombshell: Dr. Emerson is on vacation in Germany for the entire week! Seven whole days! It hit me like a ton of bricks. It feels like someone has yanked the ground out from under us. This new ENT told us straight up, "Dr. Emerson is the only surgeon who can successfully perform this surgery."

I burst into tears, and the ENT tried to offer some reassurance. Mentioning the strong IV antibiotics Collin is receiving will slow down the spread of the infection, which will buy him time until Dr. Emerson gets back.

But honestly, it felt like cold comfort in the face of this setback. I wanted to scream at him, "You know he has leukemia, right? You know his cancer treatments are delayed because of this infection, right? The antibiotics won't prevent leukemia from killing my husband!"

I insisted on getting another opinion, and the ENT agreed to call one of his colleagues to come see Collin tomorrow. I want to get off this rollercoaster of emotions! I want to wake up from this nightmare! I am beyond frustrated; I am so disheartened. How is this even possible? How is there only one surgeon who can perform this surgery? My mind is not computing this situation, but when I write things down, it helps me to process everything, so I'll keep fighting and I'll keep writing.

Day 417
February 22, 2022

Today, we met with a fourth ENT specialist, and the story was the same as before. Dr. Emerson is the only surgeon deemed skilled enough for this complex surgery. This new doctor tried to offer some comfort by saying, "If it were my family member in your situation, I would only want Dr. Emerson to perform the surgery. I wouldn't want someone to attempt a surgery they weren't comfortable with."

His words hit a nerve. I couldn't contain my frustration anymore. I snapped and yelled at him, "Of course, I don't want someone unqualified to perform the surgery. But that's not the point! This is absurd! How is there only one surgeon qualified to perform this surgery? I don't care about anything else! I only care about keeping my husband alive! You're a doctor? You're trained to keep people alive? So help me keep him alive!"

I braced myself for him to lash back at me in retaliation, but instead, he met my gaze and made a promise. "Ma'am, I'm going to call Dr. Emerson in Germany. I'll send him all the records and information he needs about your husband, so he'll be ready to jump right in on Monday."

Tears welled up as I apologized for losing my composure. His assurance and proactive approach gave me a bit of hope. He promised to return tomorrow with an update on his conversation with Dr. Emerson.

In that moment of vulnerability, amidst the tears and apologies, I felt a small sense of relief wash over me. Despite the chaos and uncertainty of this horrible situation, I know many are in our corner, fighting alongside us to ensure Collin gets the care he deserves. And for that, I'm beyond grateful.

Day 418
February 23, 2022

As promised, the ENT from yesterday returned, though I still don't know his name. He relayed the conversation he had with Dr. Emerson, assuring us he's fully aware of Collin's condition and will be here first thing Monday morning to see him.

Meanwhile, because Collin can't get the Besponza, his leukemia cell count is climbing, reaching 12% today. The oncology team is keeping a close eye on it. We are all praying it doesn't climb any higher. It's a delicate balance because it's too risky for Collin to receive any chemotherapy or immunotherapy while he has this nasty infection.

The infectious disease doctor weighed in, reiterating that ideally, we'd wait the full six weeks for Collin to complete his IV antibiotic before resuming any leukemia treatment. However, she acknowledged the urgency given the rising leukemia numbers. She's considering giving him clearance sooner than six weeks, but only after the mastoidectomy surgery, understanding the critical need to address both conditions.

As if Collin isn't battling enough already, now his kidneys are showing severe damage. The nephrologist, or kidney doctor, took me aside and shared her concerns. She's worried that if Collin's kidneys don't turn around soon, dialysis will become necessary.

It's like a cruel twist of fate, piling on another layer of complexity to an already complex and dire situation. We're already dealing with so much, and the thought of dialysis feels like another mountain to climb.

Collin is aware of what's happening, but he's in so much pain. He's been battling excruciating migraines, sensitivity to light, nausea, and vomiting, leaving him pretty much out of it. I constantly tell him how proud of him I am, and how much I appreciate how hard he is fighting. I promise him that I will fight equally hard, and that is what I am doing. Despite all these overwhelming developments, we're facing this head-on, clinging to hope with every ounce of strength we have.

Day 419
February 24, 2022

Today was a doozy. I don't know when we are going to catch a break. I always aim to arrive at the hospital early, usually before 7:00 am, to catch up with each doctor during their rounds. This morning, I arrived around 6:45 am, just as the nurses were changing shifts and gathered at the nurses' station.

Upon entering Collin's room, I heard the unsettling sound of his monitors beeping incessantly. Rushing to his bedside, I found him asleep with his oxygen mask on the floor. His oxygen saturation was low, and his heart rate was elevated, triggering the alarms. Naturally, I was upset to find his mask off, with no one monitoring him. I quickly replaced the mask over his face, whispering to him, "Good morning, Collin. It's just me. I'm putting your oxygen back on."

He stirred gently, opening his eyes, and offering a sweet greeting, "Hey, Babe. You look beautiful this morning. I'm so glad you're here." As he spoke, I noticed a slurring in his words, prompting concern. I removed the oxygen mask, hoping the slurring was because of the mask, and then I asked him about his night. He responded to my question, but his speech remained slurred. Worried, I asked him to smile for me, and when he did, the left side of his face did not move.

Immediately, I replaced his mask and raced out of the room into the hall, yelling, "I need help in here! I think Collin is having a stroke!" Within seconds, his nurse arrived. She assessed him and promptly called a stroke code. Immediately, the stroke code team flooded into the room, assessing Collin's condition before whisking him away for a CT scan.

There I stood scared and alone in the room, but having worked in the intensive care unit, I knew the protocol, and I was grateful for such a quick response. I tried to reassure myself that he was in capable hands. Forty-five minutes later, they brought him back. The CT scan revealed a blood clot in the lateral sinus vein of his head. This is terrifying, but thankfully, it's treatable with blood thinners.

The neurologist explained that the clot likely formed because of mastoiditis, the bone infection we're awaiting Dr. Emerson to perform surgery on. My thoughts keep replaying in my mind relating to the fact that if Dr. Emerson was here, this wouldn't have happened. Collin wouldn't be getting sicker before my eyes. I'm so overwhelmed. Just when I thought this nightmare couldn't get any worse, it has.

Collin's kidneys show no signs of improvement today. His leukemia cells are climbing, today they are at 36%, and I am terrified. However, I swallow my fear and put on a brave face for him. Every day feels like a battle against an unseen enemy. I pray fervently that the leukemia doesn't spiral out of control, but the hits just keep coming. Focusing on gratitude is hard, but I'm trying. I'm thankful I arrived early and noticed the issue right away. Though upset about the mask on the floor, it ultimately led to the discovery of the problem. I feel like I am surrounded by darkness, but I'm clinging to these glimmers of light.

Day 420
February 25, 2022

The leukemia cell count continues to climb, it is 42%, and the kidney doctor said Collin probably will have to start dialysis within the next day or two if his kidneys don't start improving. Meanwhile, Collin continues to endure unbearable pain. Witnessing his suffering, which surpasses the limits of what any human should have to endure, is gut-wrenching.

Adding insult to injury, I received a discouraging call today from the bone transplant coordinator at Southeastern Memorial. It turns out that none of Collin's siblings are a match for the bone marrow transplant. This news is incredibly disappointing for all of us. However, the coordinator reassured me that there is still hope for a public donor. She has already input Collin's data into the national registry to start the search.

My prayers are for Collin, his kidneys, Dr. Emerson's safe travels back to the United States, a donor match, and more miracles.

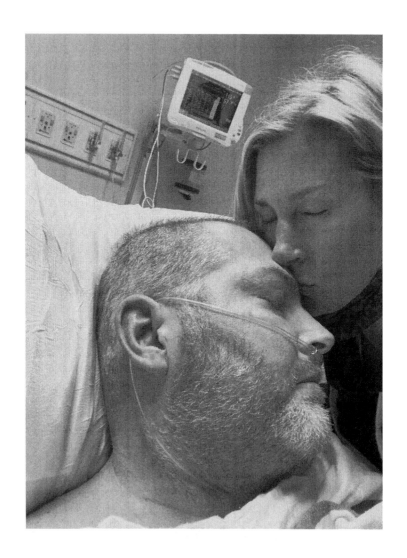

Day 421
February 26, 2022

Collin's leukemia is rapidly multiplying, reaching a frightening 52% today. His kidneys show no signs of improvement, and now there's another complication. The neurologist conducted a repeat CT scan to monitor the blood clot in his head, which thankfully remains stable. However, today's scan revealed a small brain bleed! My heart aches for Collin. With everything he's enduring; the bone infection, the blood clot, and now the brain bleed. No wonder he has been experiencing relentless migraines.

Yesterday when we discovered the blood clot, he was immediately started on blood thinners to dissolve it. But now, with the brain bleed, he has to stop the blood thinners, so the bleed doesn't get worse. The doctors are closely monitoring the clot while managing the bleeding.

To complicate matters further, Collin's blood pressure is soaring, posing an increased risk for worsening clots and additional bleeding. The nurses are doing their best to control his blood pressure, administering rescue doses of medication, but they are so busy that they aren't monitoring him the way he needs. So, I'm doing it myself. The weight of this situation is soul-crushing; I am overwhelmed and so exhausted. I don't think I've had more than an hour or two of consecutive sleep all week. Despite the commotion of people coming in and out, and the noise of the monitors, I try to get little naps here and there at the hospital, but it's almost impossible.

The doctors and nurses have expressed concern for my well-being, frequently asking if I'm taking care of myself—eating, sleeping, and taking mental breaks. I always find myself not being entirely truthful, telling them I am, even though I'm not really. It's hard to focus on my own needs when Collin needs me. I don't want to look back on this time and have any regrets.

Any time I spend away from Collin, I am going to spend with the boys. I still have to parent our four children. Thankfully, my mom and Collin's mom have been tag-teaming at the house. They've been taking turns flying into town every couple of weeks and taking care of our children, overseeing everything at home so that I can be at the hospital every day. I wouldn't be able to do this without them.

It's truly miraculous how much they've been able to handle. They aren't young—my mom is 79 years old, and Collin's mom is 70 years old. Taking care of four active boys, running a household, and tending to our puppy Echo, all while going up and down the stairs multiple times a day, is no small feat. I know it leaves them exhausted each day. Somehow, they both have found the energy to travel back and forth to Florida; my mom lives in California, and Collin's mom is in Nevada. Those are not short or easy flights, but they keep showing up to support us. Their love and dedication mean everything to me.

I'm praying fervently that Collin can endure just a little longer until Dr. Emerson arrives, just two more days. The anxiety is palpable. Every time a doctor examines

Collin, I recognize the worry in their expressions because it mirrors my own; we are all desperate to ease his suffering. Unfortunately, we can only do so much until Dr. Emerson arrives and performs the surgery. I feel like I'm going crazy, this sense of helplessness, watching Collin suffer through so much while we wait for one person. It's maddening!

Day 422
February 27, 2022

Collin's condition continues to deteriorate. This is soul-crushing. Seeing him in pain, struggling to hold on, breaks my heart into pieces. I wish I could bear this burden for him, take away his suffering, but I'm helpless.

Collin is confused and lethargic, barely waking enough to open his eyes. He mumbles his words and isn't making any sense. His kidneys are showing worsening signs of damage. He is now a week overdue for the Besponza treatment. Without it, the leukemia will completely take over, today the leukemia cell count was at 65%. Tomorrow can't come soon enough. Tomorrow Dr. Emerson is supposed to arrive.

Day 423
February 28, 2022

Today was a nightmare. We were promised Dr. Emerson would come, but he didn't show up! I am utterly spent, and I am all out of tears. It feels like every ounce of emotion has been drained from me, leaving behind a hollow ache that consumes my entire being.

Throughout the day, multiple doctors were in and out of the room. I spoke with seven different doctors, each one from a different specialty, each one with pity in their eyes. Every single one expressed the same sentiment of concern. They all assured me they are doing everything they can to help Collin, but not one of them could perform the mastoidectomy. Only Dr. Emerson can do that, and several doctors have left him messages and expressed the critical nature of the situation.

I don't understand why Dr. Emerson never came today. Maybe he doesn't understand the severity of Collin's condition (although that seems unlikely). Perhaps he doesn't care, or he got stuck in Germany. I do not know what is going on. We were all under the impression that he was going to come today. I arrived at the hospital extra early this morning because I didn't know what time he would arrive, and I wanted to make sure I was there.

I waited all day, and when he didn't come in the morning, I expected he would come during lunch or at the end of the day on his way home. But he never showed up. The leukemia is at 71% today, Collin is almost unresponsive, his kidneys are failing, the infection is still raging, and his vital signs are worsening with each passing hour.

I'm not okay. Overwhelmed by despair, I feel so helpless. But this isn't about me—it's about Collin. So, I must push aside these feelings and emotions because if I allow myself to wallow in them, I won't be able to function. I won't be able to do what I need to do to fight for the love of my life.

We need a miracle. We have witnessed many, and now I'm praying for one more.

Day 424
March 1, 2022

4:30 am: I arrive at the hospital. I tried to get a few hours of sleep at home last night, but I got zero. My mind was racing. I'm being haunted by thoughts of Collin dying because of an ear infection. An ear infection! I can't comprehend how unfortunate this whole situation is. Last night I was so defeated, that I just cried and cried, I am in despair. This is the worst feeling in the world!

8:00 am: I almost gave up, overwhelmed with defeat. But, I promised to never stop fighting for Collin, and I will keep that promise. I am determined to get Dr. Emerson here today! A quick Google search revealed the phone number for Dr. Emerson's office. I called as soon as it opened, explaining our desperate situation to anyone who would listen. The office staff informed me that Dr. Emerson will be tied up with surgeries all day, but they promised me that they would pass on my urgent message.

Then I searched for the phone number of the Director of Patient Advocacy at the hospital. I called expecting to get a voicemail, but she answered the phone! My voice trembled as tears flooded my face; I could barely articulate my words over the phone. I poured out my heart, explaining how my husband's life hung in the balance under their care and how the lack of action was jeopardizing everything we trusted the hospital to provide. To my relief, she listened with sincere compassion and empathy and offered her help in any way possible.

By 9:00 am, I had also reached out to my friend Chad. Recalling that Chad had a connection to the hospital's president, I made a desperate plea, asking him to assist me in contacting the hospital's administration. Chad, eager to help, assured me he would start making phone calls.

But I didn't stop there. I also recalled that one of my neighbors, a general contractor, was currently building the home of the hospital's CFO. He mentioned this a few months ago, offering his help if I ever encountered any issues. With desperation driving me, I reached out to my neighbor, explaining Collin's situation and the urgent need for Dr. Emerson to perform the mastoidectomy. My neighbor, also eager to help, said he would help me get in contact with his client.

12:00 pm: The oncologist pulled me into the hall, and with tears in her eyes she delivered devastating news: Collin's leukemia count has skyrocketed to 88%. She explained that she is working on getting clearance to restart the immunotherapy Besponza tomorrow. Concerned that his infection could turn deadly with Besponza, she elaborated on the complexities, stating that without it, Collin will surely die within the next few days. She inquired about any updates on Dr. Emerson's arrival. I conveyed my ongoing efforts, but stressed she still needed to keep pushing from her end. She revealed she had left several messages but had yet to receive a response from Dr. Emerson himself.

1:30 pm: As I sat by Collin's bedside, a knock on the door startled me. A woman I didn't recognize stepped inside. As she shook my hand, she handed me her business card and introduced herself. "Hello, Mrs. Jager, my name is Emily, and I am the President of the hospital. I was just informed of your situation and wanted to personally come to check on your husband and you. I also wanted to inform you that Dr. Emerson will be here this evening to examine Mr. Jager."

While I was appreciative of her visit and felt relieved by the news, I knew it wasn't enough. I couldn't hold back my frustration as I explained, "Dr. Emerson merely assessing Collin will not be sufficient. My husband is dying, and he is dying because your hospital doesn't have policies in place to ensure that patients get the care they need when a doctor goes out of the country."

Urgency laced my words as I emphasized that the surgery must happen tonight: "We have run out of time, and waiting until tomorrow is no longer an option."

She nodded in understanding, agreeing that it was a top priority. She informed me that her phone number was on her business card and promised to call me in a few hours to check in on how things were going.

2:15 pm: My phone rang. I answered. It was the Director of Patient Advocacy, the same person I spoke to this morning. She informed me that the transport team would arrive at approximately 5:00 pm to take Collin to a presurgical suite, where Dr. Emerson would assess his infection and determine the extent of surgery required. Once again, I emphasized that while I appreciated Dr. Emerson's imminent arrival, an examination wouldn't suffice; Collin needed the surgery over a week ago. I will accept nothing other than Dr. Emerson performing the surgery tonight! She acknowledged my concern and assured me she would relay the message to Dr. Emerson.

3:00 pm: A text message popped up from a local number I didn't recognize. It was the CFO of the hospital, the client of my neighbor. His message read: "Hello, Mrs. Jager, I am deeply sorry for your husband's health challenges. Please know he is in excellent hands, and we are committed to ensuring he receives the care he needs. I was informed the surgeon will be seeing him tonight. This is my personal cell phone; feel free to call or text me anytime day or night with any concerns. I am here to support you."

5:15 pm: The transport team finally arrived to take Collin to Dr. Emerson. There was no way I wasn't going to go with them, so I followed along. They took us to a presurgical room, where they typically prep patients for surgery. Dominating the space was a massive machine, one I didn't recognize, I figured it was something Dr. Emerson requested as it occupied a significant portion of the room.

After about 15 minutes of waiting, the door swung open, and in walked an older gentleman in a white lab coat. He had white hair, a slight build, and gentle eyes. He introduced himself. "Hello, I'm Dr. Emerson." At that moment, I struggled to contain my emotions. Every fiber of my being wanted to unleash a torrent of frustration: "Why did it take you so long? Why didn't you come yesterday? You might be too late!" But I held my tongue. We desperately needed him. So, I simply replied, "Thank you for coming."

Dr. Emerson examined Collin's ear using the giant machine, presumably a microscope. After his assessment, he turned to me and delivered the verdict. "Mrs. Jager, this infection is really severe. I am going to have to perform surgery tonight." As he removed his gloves, he added, "I need to make some phone calls. I need to cancel my dinner reservations and will call my physician's assistant to assist me with the surgery. I expect the surgery will take around 3 hours. But I will update you when it's all done."

Once again, I fought against the impulse to unleash my frustration and anger. I wanted to scream at him, "No kidding, you have to cancel your dinner plans! No kidding, the infection is really severe! This was an emergency last week! What do you think everybody has been trying to tell you?" But I suppressed those words, holding them back as tears streamed down my face. With a heavy heart, I simply nodded silently and whispered, "Thank you."

About five minutes later, the preoperative nurse walked into the room. She had an IV bag of fluid in her hand, a 1-liter bag of lactated Ringer's solution. Without introducing herself or acknowledging either Collin or me, she walked over to Collin's IV pump and began hooking up the fluid. Surprised by her actions, I said, "What are you doing?" She looked at me and responded, "I'm starting him on IV fluids."

I was shocked! I raised my voice and aggressively said, "Are you trying to kill him? His kidneys are failing, his body is retaining liters of extra fluid, and his blood pressure is sky-high! The absolute last thing that you should give him is extra IV fluids!"

She looked surprised and said, "This is just standard protocol. We start IV fluids on all patients before surgery." I replied sharply, "He is not a standard patient! You are not giving him those IV fluids!" Then I pointed to the vital signs monitor on the wall. "You see his blood pressure? It's 198/132! Do you want him to have a stroke? He needs an IV push of labetalol (a medication used to rapidly lower blood pressure)! Go get it now! And while you're at it, go ahead and order some platelets. His platelet count is low. He is going to need to have platelets transfused during surgery so he doesn't bleed out on the table!"

Without saying another word, she hurried out of the room. Within minutes, she returned with another nurse. She had the labetalol, and the other nurse had the platelets. Their prompt response made me feel a tinge of relief. I said apologetically, "I'm sorry I yelled at you." Then I cried, "This is my husband, he is my world. And he has almost died on me many times. I am so scared, I can't let him die. I won't be able to survive without him."

The first nurse looked at me and said, "No, please don't apologize. I am so glad you are here to inform me. I didn't have any orders for him. He wasn't on the surgery schedule. Dr. Emerson just came out of the room and told me to 'get him prepped for surgery'. I didn't know his history, or anything about him."

Then the second nurse said, "Are you a doctor? A nurse?" I replied, "I'm a nurse." She reassured me, "If this was someone I loved, I would be the same way. You are doing exactly what you should do, and you should be proud of yourself. Your husband is lucky to have you."

I thanked them repeatedly, they both hugged me and promised they would take good care of Collin.

6:20 pm: The surgical nurse came in and said it was time for the surgery. She confirmed my phone number and advised me to go home, reminding me that Dr. Emerson would call me once the surgery was complete.

Leaving the hospital, I felt a mix of relief and complete exhaustion. Today has been one of the hardest days of my life. When I got home, I crawled straight into bed with my puppy and melted into the sheets. Overwhelmed by everything that had happened, I sobbed into my pillows. I don't know how much more Collin can handle. I don't know how much more I can handle. This is all too hard.

11:55 pm: My phone rang. I anxiously answered the phone, expecting it to be Dr. Emerson. I could tell he was driving, and I could sense the exhaustion in his voice as he spoke. He explained that the surgery took much longer than expected. The infection had spread extensively, requiring the removal of a significant portion of bone. Collin's low platelet count posed additional challenges, as he had lost a considerable amount of blood during the procedure, making it difficult for him to navigate and perform the surgery. However, despite these challenges, Dr. Emerson reassured me that the surgery was ultimately a success.

Day 425
March 2, 2022

I finally feel a sense of relief, as if someone has lifted a little weight off my chest. Collin is more awake and alert today, and the surgery has eased some of his migraine pain. However, he is still confused and disoriented with slurred speech. Despite the leukemia count being 88%, he was able to get out of bed and sit in a chair for fifteen minutes! Now that the mastoidectomy is complete, it's time to get back to attacking the leukemia.

Collin got his dose of Besponza this morning, and with it comes a bunch of serious side effects. Especially concerning is the delay in healing of the surgical wound and the increased risk of worsening infection. We don't even know if it will successfully kill the leukemia, but it's our only option, so we are moving forward.

Additionally, Collin's kidneys have shown no improvement, his whole body is extremely swollen, and he will start dialysis today. But despite all of this, Collin hasn't stopped fighting, and he hasn't stopped smiling. Notice the half smile and his facial paralysis on his left side, caused by the blood clot in his head. He continues to be the light that shines in the darkness. I don't know what I did to deserve this man, but I am forever grateful that he is mine.

Day 426
March 3, 2022

The Besponza is working. Overnight, Collin's leukemia count dropped to 55%! I am so relieved to see him making progress.

Collin's kidneys are still not properly filtering as they should, and despite being on dialysis, there is a buildup of toxins in his bloodstream, which has been affecting his brain function. For over a week, he's struggled with slurred speech and confusion because of this condition. However, tonight was different. As I was telling him goodnight, he suddenly became very coherent (for the first time all week) and he said clearly with confidence, "I need everyone to pray for my kidneys, specifically. And if they do, I believe my kidneys will be healed, just like my liver was."

In that moment, I looked into my husband's eyes and witnessed his look of determination and belief. I whispered with a smile, "You my Love, are a miracle."

I know miracles are indeed possible, and sometimes, the greatest miracles are the ones we never saw coming.

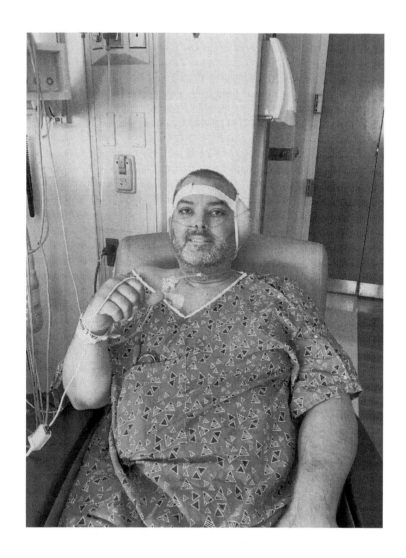

Day 429
March 6, 2022

Collin's remarkable recovery is nothing short of amazing. Today brought incredible news: his kidneys are on the mend, and there's a chance that today could be his final dialysis session! His mental clarity has returned; he has been working with the speech therapist, and his speech is becoming clearer each day. The Besponza treatment is working wonders, with the leukemia numbers dropping to 26% today. And to top it all off, he even took a walk around the unit today with the aid of a walker. Every day, I am so inspired by him!

Day 432
March 9, 2022

Miracles continue to unfold! Collin's healing and gaining strength. If things keep progressing this way, he might go home in a few days! I can't believe it. Seriously, I didn't think this would be a possibility a week ago.

Today he received intrathecal chemotherapy, which is chemotherapy injected directly into the cerebrospinal fluid. The procedure involves inserting a needle into the spinal column through a space in the lower back. Over the last 15 months, he has had this procedure eleven times. Collin hates this procedure. It's awfully painful, and it leaves him with a severe headache and nausea, but every time he faces it with a bravery that never fails to humble me.

Day 434
March 11, 2022

We are so excited; Collin gets to come home today! I am offering prayers of appreciation for the multiple blessings that have been poured upon our family and the many miracles we have witnessed.

Day 437
March 14, 2022

When Collin relapsed in January of this year, after being on maintenance chemotherapy for just two months, I felt devastated beyond words. My knees buckled, and I collapsed on the hospital floor and cried like I had never cried before. The weight of the situation was unbearable. Knowing the pain he would have to endure and the fear of losing him were agonizing. And beneath it all lay the stark realization that my journey as a 24/7 caregiver was far from over. Over the past 434 days, my spirit has been broken more times than I can say, leaving me emotionally, physically, and mentally depleted. Each day, I struggle to keep up with the relentless demands placed on me.

But today, I finally glimpsed a faint light at the end of a very long, dark tunnel. Today, we received the news that Collin has not one, but two full-match donors identified through the national registry! Today, hope found me. Hope that the healing miracle we've been fervently praying for, to eradicate leukemia from Collin's body once and for all, may become a reality.

We still have a challenging journey ahead, but today, my broken spirit was mended. And I am certain, no matter how many times my spirit breaks, it will always be restored and made whole again. This is the promise the Lord has given to me.

Chapter Eight

Bone Marrow Transplant

A bone marrow transplant is a medical procedure where doctors replace unhealthy bone marrow with healthy bone marrow from a donor. Bone marrow is like a factory inside our bones that makes blood cells, including red blood cells that carry oxygen, white blood cells that fight infections, and platelets that help our blood clot.

For a patient like Collin, who is fighting acute lymphoblastic leukemia (ALL), the bone marrow becomes overwhelmed and produces an excessive amount of immature white blood cells called lymphoblasts. These crowd out the healthy blood cells, leaving him very sick and weak.

This is where the bone marrow transplant comes in. During this procedure, healthy bone marrow from a donor will be given to Collin intravenously, much like a blood transfusion. Once the new bone marrow takes root in Collin's body, it gets to work, producing healthy blood cells. These new cells can help combat any remaining leukemia and rebuild Collin's weakened immune system.

For Collin, this bone marrow transplant isn't just a medical procedure—it's his chance for a new beginning, a fresh start. It's his ticket to kicking leukemia to the curb and being cancer-free. However, it's a big procedure with many risks and challenges. Collin will need to continue being brave and strong, and his dedicated medical team will closely monitor him.

Day 441
March 18, 2022

This morning began like any other. I administered Collin's morning medications, checked his vital signs, and assessed how he was feeling. He told me he felt okay, not great, but okay. I had planned to take him to a routine appointment at Jackson Miller outpatient clinic for blood tests and a check-in with Dr. Larson. Collin told me he wanted to shower before the appointment. Though I had purchased a shower chair for him last year, he prefers not to use it, feeling it undermines his independence. Because of his unstable condition, I usually stand close by when he showers, ready to assist if needed. As he began to shower, I noticed his breathing was heavy, a sign that set off alarm bells in my mind. Concerned, I asked if he was okay. He said he was okay, but admitted he was feeling weaker than normal. This increased my worry.

Thankfully, Ian was nearby in the other room. I quickly called out to him to bring the shower chair for Collin to use. Ian misunderstood my request and brought a metal bar stool instead. I made do, urging Collin to sit down. As I began washing his back, disaster struck! His eyes rolled into the back of his head, and his whole body got tense and stiff, and then, in the very next second, his body went limp. Instinctively, to keep him from falling off the stool, I wrapped my arms around him.

Then I yelled out for Ian, screaming, "Ian, call 911! Dad passed out in the shower!"

I struggled to keep Collin's body upright. He is much larger than me, over twice my size and three times my weight, and to make matters worse, he was wet and slippery. "Collin, are you okay? Collin, talk to me!" I yelled desperately, but there was no response. All I heard were scary gurgling noises coming from his mouth, and then he vomited.

Ian rushed into the bathroom, his voice trembling as he spoke to the 911 dispatcher on the phone. I instructed Ian to turn on the speakerphone and to bring it close to me so I could speak to the dispatcher while maintaining my grip on Collin. I tried my best to remain calm as I relayed our address and explained the situation. Urgency dripped from every word. "Please, hurry! Please send someone to help!" I pleaded.

The dispatcher assured me that the fire department was on its way. The dispatcher instructed Ian to go outside to the front of our house and flag down the fire truck upon arrival.

I was left alone with Collin in the shower. I clung onto him for dear life, the weight of his limp body bearing down on me. It became increasingly difficult to keep him upright, and the thought of him falling onto the hard

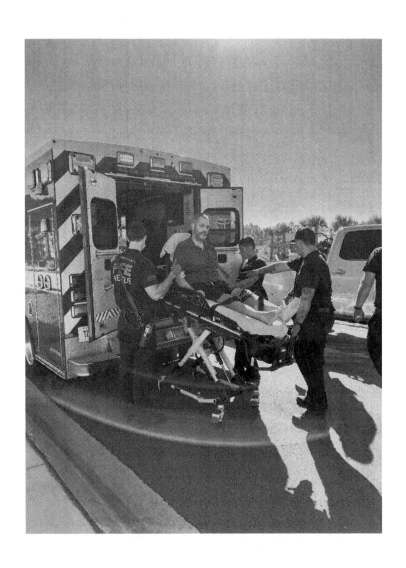

shower floor played on repeat in my mind. Knowing that his platelet levels are dangerously low, I understood that any fall could have fatal consequences. I was determined not to let him fall.

"Collin, wake up! Please, wake up!" I pleaded, my voice full of fear and desperation. Every fiber of my being urged him to regain consciousness. With each passing second, the stakes grew higher, and my cries for him to awaken echoed off the tiled walls of the bathroom.

Finally, after what seemed like hours, but in reality, was only about three minutes, he lifted his head and started to talk. He was confused and didn't know what was going on. Relieved that he woke up, I was still not loosening my grip on him for fear that he would pass out again; I explained to him what happened, and I assured him help was on the way.

A few tense minutes later, the firemen arrived. I allowed them to take over, grateful they were there. But just as soon as they took over, Collin passed out again! The second time was shorter than the first, and thankfully, when he woke up, he seemed more aware of the situation. Collin assured everyone he was fine and insisted on getting dressed. With my help, he was able to get some clothes on, and then the firemen quickly got him onto a gurney and rushed him to the emergency room.

Now, we're here in the emergency room. Thankfully, he hasn't passed out for a third time. Since we've been at the hospital, he's been awake, alert, and coherent, which is a tremendous relief. He says he remembers being in the shower and not feeling good, but he remembers nothing after that.

The doctor ordered a bunch of tests to figure out what's going on, but we're still waiting for answers. I have a feeling Collin's going to end up getting admitted to the hospital. He really doesn't want to stay overnight. He has so much trauma from being in the hospital. But I'm not comfortable bringing him home, not until he's had a couple of days free from any more episodes.

Today was shocking and terrifying. Collin has never done anything like that before. I can't help but wonder what could have happened if I hadn't been there. Or if Ian hadn't been close by to bring me the stool, or call 911. This could have had a devastating outcome. I'm truly grateful for the miraculous way everything unfolded, and I'm so thankful that Collin is still here with us.

Day 444
March 18, 2022

Collin is being discharged from the hospital today. After Friday's incident, the doctors wanted to monitor him over the weekend. All the tests have returned as normal, therefore, the cause of his passing out remains unknown. This hospital admission turned out to be surprisingly quite boring, which I wholeheartedly welcome! Boring equals easy—we've had enough excitement to last a lifetime!

Collin was in relatively good spirits this weekend. With limited options to pass the time in the hospital, we made the most of it by taking walks around the oncology floor, watching movies, and engaging in quiet conversations. Despite the ease of this admission, the hospital environment lacks privacy, it's loud, and the food is horrible. Most of Collin's meals during his hospital stays come from either food I bring from home or orders placed through a food delivery service. The nurse assistants are always so sweet; when I'm unable to retrieve Collin's food delivery order from the hospital entrance, they gladly go fetch it for him.

We are so relieved that everything seems to be okay, and our family is excited to all be back together under the same roof.

Day 447
March 24, 2022

Collin and I had another meeting with the bone marrow transplant team at Southeastern Memorial today. They've been in touch with the donor, who has agreed to travel to Southeastern Memorial the first week of April for the bone marrow cell collection procedure. Shortly after, they will admit Collin to the hospital for pre-bone marrow conditioning. The preconditioning regimen will last about four to five days. During this time, Collin will receive chemotherapy to completely eliminate his own bone marrow in preparation for receiving the donor's marrow.

The doctors have emphasized the intense nature of the bone marrow transplant process, warning us of potential complications, before and after the transplant, including death. Because of these risks, Collin has had several medical appointments and health screenings to assess his suitability and tolerance for the procedure. So far, cardiology, pulmonology, and psychology has cleared him, infectious disease will provide clearance once he completes six weeks of IV antibiotics for the mastoiditis infection. He's in week five, so next week he will complete the six weeks of antibiotics.

Both Collin and I are nervous about the transplant. There are so many moving parts and so many things out of our control, but we are hopeful and excited to move forward, knowing this is Collin's best chance of survival.

I am filled with immense love and gratitude for Collin's donor. Everything in the donor process is completely anonymous. We know nothing about them—not their sex, age, or whereabouts, and vice versa. I wish I could hug them and express my appreciation for the selflessness of their act. However, there's hope for connection in the future. If both the donor and Collin agree, the transplant center will facilitate written communication a year after the transplant, with the possibility of an in-person meeting two years later. Oh, how I look forward to that day!

Day 448
March 25, 2022

Collin returned to the hospital after only being home for four days. His midline IV, which I use for administering his IV antibiotics at home for mastoiditis, has become painful, red, and he developed a fever this morning, indicating a possible infection. The medical team decided to remove the midline IV, and upon removal, they found a blood clot on the end, which could be the cause of the symptoms.

However, we need to be sure, therefore, the doctors ordered a full septic workup. Collin will remain in the hospital for at least 48 hours until the cultures come back, hopefully negative with no growth. Though it's a setback, as long as there's no infection, it shouldn't affect the bone marrow transplant timeline.

My heart goes out to Collin—he absolutely dreads being back in the hospital. His anxiety is through the roof, and he practically pleaded with me not to call the doctor when his fever spiked. It's tough seeing him struggle like this, especially knowing how much he hates the isolating atmosphere of the hospital. He hates being away from our children; it's heartbreaking for him. I've noticed his mood sinking deeper into depression with each hospital stay.

Despite it all, we're trying to stay positive. During the car ride to the hospital, we listed all the tender mercies we saw today. There were dozens. We're both exhausted, but we're choosing to continue to look for the light. This is how we find strength to keep going.

Day 450
March 27, 2022

Great news! Collin's cultures came back clean, indicating no infection, therefore he was able to return home. He had a new midline placed. I'll continue administering his IV antibiotics until the end of this week, and then hopefully we can put the mastoiditis behind us for good!

Collin does have to return to Jackson Miller Medical Institute next week for another hospital stay. He will be receiving another round of Besponsa immunotherapy in hopes of keeping the leukemia below 5%. If all goes as planned, that stay will last five days. Shortly after, he will be admitted to Southeastern Memorial Hospital to begin chemotherapy to prep his body for the bone marrow transplant!

The closer we get to the transplant, the more nervous and excited I get!

Day 458
April 4, 2022

We got some distressing news today. The bone marrow donor was scheduled to fly in this week for collection. The Southeastern Memorial transplant coordinator called me today and told me the donor had a conflict and canceled at the last minute! We do not know when they will be available to come. We are praying it will be soon. That is the only information I have, because the donor must remain anonymous the transplant coordinator couldn't tell me anything else.

I'm trying to not be frustrated, but I am. Collin has fought so hard, and I just don't want to see him suffer anymore. Today was Collin's scheduled admission at Jackson Miller for the Besponsa treatment. The Jackson Miller oncology team is trying to be encouraging, telling us they will administer another round of Besponsa after this round, while Collin waits for the donor to be available. But with the donor setback, it feels like we're grasping for temporary solutions. I know the Besponsa is just a temporary band-aid fix. The leukemia has shown it's aggressive, and it's smart. I can't shake the fear of it becoming resistant to the Besponsa while we wait for the donor.

Collin is taking the news like a champ. He holds onto a firm belief that whatever is meant to be will unfold in its own time. He told me, "It's out of our hands, we need to trust in God's timing." Collin is right; he is always right. Sometimes it's just really hard to remain patient and keep the faith.

Day 461
April 7, 2022

It's been three days since I talked to the transplant coordinator at Southeastern Memorial. I'm not the most patient person in the world, so I called her for an update. Had she talked to the donor? Do we have a new collection date? The coordinator told me she had been reaching out to the donor but had not been able to get in contact with them. She reassured me we still have a second donor who is also a full match; she said if she hadn't heard from donor #1 in the next few days, she would reach out to donor #2.

I boldly told her I didn't think she should wait a few days, and I would like her to reach out to donor #2 today. I'm not sure what the protocol is in a situation like this, but we don't have time to waste.

Collin is still in the hospital for monitoring post his Besponsa treatment. So far, he has tolerated it well and should be discharged home tomorrow.

Day 465
April 11, 2022

I have called the transplant coordinator every day, hoping for a bit of good news. She has tried to contact donor #1 multiple times and has received no response. Even donor #2 remains elusive, leaving us in a race against time. My thoughts swirl with questions about why donor #1 canceled, why they haven't returned calls, and the reasons behind it all.

I am trying not to be angry, but I am. I recognize that this anger stems from pain, it stems from fear. My mind is reeling, and the uncertainty and frustration is bringing up a lot of trauma. I don't want to go back to that place where I watched Collin slowly slipping away, helpless to do anything to stop it.

Collin is continuing to endure with remarkable patience. He is constantly teaching me to be better, to do better.

He inspires me every day. I tell him this often. I don't know what I did to get so lucky to call him mine, but every day he is my guiding light.

Day 466
April 12, 2022

Today we got good news and bad news. The bad news is donor #1 can no longer donate. The good news is that donor #2 is ready to come donate their bone marrow cells the first week of May. Dr. Raymond, Collin's transplant oncologist, advised against any further immunotherapy or chemotherapy before his admission for the transplant. Given the toll these treatments have taken on his body, it's crucial to allow him time to recover and build up strength before the transplant. This decision makes me nervous. Collin's Besponsa treatments have been exactly 4 weeks apart, and we are going to be pushing right at that timeline. But, I trust the expertise of the medical team, and I am choosing to focus on the positives and the certainties in this situation.

The plan is for Collin to be admitted on May 4th, with the donor cells scheduled for collection on May 9th. Then, on May 11th, Collin will undergo the transplant procedure! One day after my birthday, the best gift I could ask for!

This week and next are filled with appointments and tests to make sure Collin's body is strong enough to handle the transplant process. We pray that all goes smoothly, and we have no more setbacks. We are ready to get this transplant party started!

Day 480
April 26, 2022

The last two weeks have been hectic, with lots and lots of doctor's appointments. A few days ago, we received the results of Collin's latest bone marrow biopsy, and it showed less than 1% leukemia cells. We are thrilled with this news!

Unfortunately, with cancer, the rollercoaster of emotions never stops; disappointment quickly followed the good news. Yesterday, an abdominal MRI showed what appears to be clusters of leukemia that have spread from Collin's liver to his pancreas, kidneys, spleen, and thoracic spine. Of course, this is not the news we were hoping for. He will need to have a biopsy to confirm that it is leukemia.

Despite this, Collin's spirits are up and he is feeling fairly strong. I'm trying not to freak out, and not go down rabbit holes of terrible possibilities. But the idea that the leukemia might be spreading to new areas of Collin's body fills me with so much anxiety and fear.

Collin keeps reminding me to focus on the good, and to cling to the belief that better days are ahead.

Day 487
May 3, 2022

My heart is heavy. We met with Dr. Raymond, Collin's oncologist, at Southeastern Memorial today, and we were quite surprised by the news he gave us. Collin's bone marrow transplant has been postponed indefinitely.

As I previously explained, his abdominal MRI showed that his leukemia might have spread to his liver and other surrounding organs. He will have a biopsy tomorrow to give us a definitive diagnosis, but regardless of the liver biopsy results, Collin is still showing leukemia in his bone marrow. Even though it's a small amount, <1% of leukemia cells, Dr. Raymond wants no detectable leukemia cells before they proceed with the bone marrow transplant. Typically, for a transplant to occur, the patient needs to have <5% of detectable leukemia cells. But since Collin's body is so beaten and battered from round after round of aggressive chemotherapy, Dr. Raymond needs his body to be stronger and show zero leukemia for the bone marrow transplant to be successful.

My emotions are all over the place. I don't even know how to articulate my feelings into words. Constantly changing and adapting to new plans and dealing with perpetual uncertainty is difficult and frustrating. It feels like our lives have been spinning out of control for so long, it's hard to remember what life felt like before cancer ruled it.

I am very overwhelmed, and I'm trying to process everything. But this is the new plan: Collin is going to receive CAR-T cell therapy. CAR-T cell therapy is a type of immunotherapy that will use Collin's own T cells (a type of immune system cell), to attack and kill the leukemia cells. The medical team will extract Collin's T cells from his blood and then send them to a specialized lab where they will genetically modify them into soldier cells known as CAR-T cells. Then Collin will get them infused back into his body. The hope is that these CAR-T cells will attack and destroy all remaining leukemia in his body.

The CAR-T cell process is much more involved than I have explained. It is extremely risky and has potentially fatal side effects. This process will take a toll on his body, and he will need a few months to recover. Once the CAR-T cells have successfully destroyed the leukemia and his body has time to regain strength, we can proceed with a bone marrow transplant.

Collin's transplant team thoroughly discussed the decision to delay the bone marrow transplant. All five hematology doctors at Southeastern Memorial (who all specialize in bone marrow transplants and CAR-T cell therapy) agreed that this new plan is his best chance of survival.

I know Collin is worried. Continuously, he reassures me that everything will be fine and that everything will work out. He always puts on a brave face and tries to be strong for me. But when he gets quiet, I know he is feeling the weight of it. He and I are opposites. I like to purge my feelings and emotions, and he internalizes them. But no matter how we process our emotions, it's extremely difficult to find the balance between acknowledging the reality of our situation and finding the strength to keep moving forward when it feels like the very fabric of our world is constantly unraveling.

The only thing we can do is try our best. Together we have agreed to trust the experts and to continue to put 100% of our trust and faith in God. We know He is mindful of our family, aware of our struggles and fears, and without a doubt, loves us unconditionally. We will continue to fight, seeking the light every day. Perspective can change everything. As long as we have each other, we will face each challenge hand in hand. And with every new dawn, we will find the strength to rise again.

Chapter Nine

CAR-T Cell Therapy

Trying to control the uncontrollable is an exhausting feat. I hate that things are progressing this way, and I hate how I cannot take this burden from him. Every day, I try a little harder to trust the process. The next step in the process is CAR-T cell therapy. It will take a few weeks to transform Collin's T cells into CAR-T cells. Here's a general outline of the steps involved:

1) T Cell Harvesting: The doctor will extract T cells from Collin's blood through a vein in his neck using a procedure called leukapheresis. The blood will be passed through a machine that collects the T cells, and then the rest of the blood will be returned to Collin. The procedure is expected to take about eight hours, and it will be performed as an outpatient procedure.

2) Transport to the Laboratory: The harvested T cells will then be transported to a specialized laboratory in Southern California, where they will undergo genetic modification to become CAR-T cells.

3) Genetic Modification: In the laboratory, the T cells are genetically modified to express chimeric antigen receptors (CARs) on their surface. The cells are then cultured and expanded to increase their numbers. By

introducing CARs into T cells, they are engineered to recognize and target specific proteins on the leukemia cells, thereby enhancing their ability to attack and destroy the cancer cells once they are infused back into Collin's body.

4) Quality Control: Once the genetic modification is complete, the CAR-T cells undergo rigorous testing to ensure that they meet quality and safety standards. This includes testing for purity, potency, and the absence of contaminants.

5) Transport Back to the Hospital: After passing quality control, the CAR-T cells will then be transported back to Southeastern Memorial Hospital for Collin's treatment.

6) Infusion: Finally, the CAR-T cells will be ready to be infused back into Collin's bloodstream. This typically takes a few hours and requires hospitalization to monitor for potential side effects. If all goes well, he will remain in the hospital for a minimum of two weeks for monitoring and side effect symptom management.

Day 490
May 6, 2022

Today hit me hard. We received biopsy results; it confirmed the leukemia has infiltrated not just the liver, but also the pancreas, kidneys, spleen, and even the thoracic spine. It is spreading fast, causing lots of damage. However, the doctors have assured us that once Collin's body is rid of all leukemia, these vital organs can heal themselves. Therefore, our number one priority remains unchanged: we must eradicate every leukemia cell, as it is the source of all disease right now.

Since Collin's relapse in January, he has been receiving Besponsa immunotherapy every four weeks. But I am nervous, because as of today, it has been exactly four and a half weeks since his last Besponsa treatment. With no planned Besponsa treatments scheduled, I am so worried that the leukemia will rapidly multiply and everything will spin out of control again.

I have expressed this concern to both Dr. Raymond and Dr. Larson, and they both explained to me that Collin cannot receive any more immunotherapy or chemotherapy until his T cells are harvested because those medications will wipe out his T cells, effectively making collection impossible.

In addition, each time Collin receives Besponsa, it has a cumulative impact on his body. If it's feasible, they would like to avoid Collin receiving any more immunotherapy or chemotherapy. The doctors need Collin to be in the best physical condition possible before receiving the CAR-T cells, as they believe he will have a higher chance of success the physically stronger he is.

We have no alternative but to move forward with CAR-T cell therapy, and if Collin requires more Besponsa, his T cells must be harvested before he can receive it. But I'm stressed because the cells won't be collected for another week!

Southeastern Memorial will send Collin's T cells to a lab in Southern California after harvesting them. Once they are at the lab, it will take about three weeks for the cells to transform, and then they will get transported back to Southeastern Memorial.

During the week of May 30th, Collin will be admitted to Southeastern Memorial to prepare his body for the CAR-T cells. This preparation will include three consecutive days of chemotherapy. Which will effectively wipe out all of his current T cells and replace them with CAR-T cells. This is a newer type of cancer treatment, but the doctors said it can be very effective; we are encouraged by the potential of these CAR-T cells to be the miracle we desperately need.

Even though today's news was rough, Collin continues to smile. One thing he frequently says to me when I get worried is, "We've witnessed too many miracles for them to stop now."

Day 491
May 7, 2022

In January, Rosario reached out to me, asking for permission to organize the Lace Up for Collin 5K race again this year. Honestly, I felt hesitant, not because we did not appreciate the race last year, but because I was worried about how people might perceive it. I did not want people to think we were seeking attention or sympathy. When I shared these concerns with Rosario, she reassured me that my worries were unnecessary. She emphasized that it was an honor for her, as well as the other volunteers and participants, to show their love and support for us.

Her words helped me see things from a different perspective. I realized that allowing the race to take place wasn't about seeking attention or placing a burden on others; it's about embracing the love and support that surrounds us. It's about allowing others to support Collin and our family in a way that brings people together and fosters a sense of unity and connection. Ultimately, Rosario's reassurances and perspective helped to ease my hesitancy. With her encouragement and my new understanding, I felt more confident in granting permission for allowing the race to take place.

Rosario quickly started working on event planning, and the race took place this morning. Collin has not been feeling well. He has been extremely weak, and I honestly wasn't expecting him to attend. But he woke up this morning and said he wanted to at least try to make an appearance, and shockingly, he was able to stay for the entire race! It took a tremendous amount of energy for him to attend, but seeing him there, smiling and socializing with people, filled me with an overwhelming sense of pride and admiration. Despite the difficulties he faces, Collin continues to show kindness, and love to everyone around him.

Today's event was a delightful distraction from the chaos that is our life. As I navigated the crowd, I felt touched and had immense gratitude for the overwhelming outpouring of support and the tangible sense of love that our community continues to show for us.

Day 493
May 9, 2022

I am so frustrated, I could scream. Exactly what I worried about happening is happening! After the race on Saturday, Collin was utterly exhausted. He was grateful to attend, but the event completely wiped him out. On Sunday, he began complaining of more aches and pains; it seemed more than usual. I am always on high alert, so I took his temperature, but he didn't have a fever. Since it was the weekend, I waited until today, Monday, to call the doctor to order blood work.

First thing this morning, I called his doctor and requested labs. Unfortunately, the blood work revealed 5% leukemia blasts. When I heard this news, my heart dropped because I knew we couldn't afford to wait over four weeks for another Besponsa treatment!

The Southeastern Memorial team promptly consulted with the Jackson Miller team and decided to move forward with the T cell collection on Friday. We have to wait four more days. After harvesting the cells at Southeastern Memorial, I will take him to Jackson Miller Hospital for admission and to receive more Besponsa immunotherapy and chemotherapy.

It makes things more hectic, going back and forth between the two different hospitals. But considering that Collin has received all previous chemotherapy and immunotherapy treatments at Jackson Miller, it only makes sense for him to continue with his treatments there before transitioning to CAR-T cell therapy at Southeastern Memorial.

I know Collin has a team of doctors from two prestigious cancer centers overseeing his treatments, but this plan terrifies me. I'm absolutely terrified the leukemia will spiral out of control in the next five days. Watching Collin suffer through this before was so traumatic - it's seared into my mind, and I can't bear the thought of either of us going through that hell again. Because of these fears, I asked Dr. Raymond if we could collect Collin's T cells sooner, since they can only administer Besponsa after the collection procedure. But unfortunately, Friday is the soonest they can accommodate him.

To add to all this stress, Collin is feeling very anxious about being readmitted to the hospital. He is scared because he remembers the pain from the last time his leukemia blast count was high. I don't blame him; I am also stressed. But I am doing my best to remain positive and hopeful for him. I reminded him how blessed we are to have top experts from two of the country's leading hospitals weighing in on his care.

Day 496
May 12, 2022

I am in full panic mode! Three days ago, Collin's leukemia blast count was 5% and today it skyrocketed to 29%! Leukemia is aggressively taking over, and I could not contain my frustration when I confronted Dr. Raymond today.

"I told you he couldn't wait this long between treatments! I knew it! You waited too long! And now it might be too late!" I blurted out, the fear, frustration, and desperation were all-consuming, and I couldn't hold them back. He must be well-versed in dealing with upset family members, because he calmly but firmly reminded me that CAR-T cell therapy is Collin's best and only option at this point. He reiterated that we have no choice but to continue with the plan.

His calm demeanor served as a counterbalance to my frantic energy, and in that moment, I had to dig deep and draw upon inner reserves of strength and resilience. I couldn't let panic and fear consume me entirely. I have to focus on what needs to be done to fight for Collin.

Adding to the complexity, Collin's left ear, the one that previously caused all the drama, is once again causing him pain. After reaching out to Dr. Emerson, the ENT surgeon, we discovered through a CT scan that his bone infection has returned and is causing more damage! I am sobbing as I write this. When is this nightmare going to end? When are we going to get a break?

Collin is weak; he is in pain, he is nauseous, he is exhausted. I am exhausted. Words cannot express how frustrating it is that we are almost five hundred days into this horrible nightmare, and I feel like we are back at square one!

In the past ten hours alone, I have made at least a dozen phone calls and talked to a half a dozen doctors. Now, finally, we have a solid plan in place. Tomorrow morning, Southeastern Memorial will collect Collin's T-cells, which will be an eight-hour process. From there, I will rush him over to Jackson Miller Medical Institute for admission, where he'll receive IV antibiotics for the bone infection and Besponsa for the leukemia.

Today was grueling. I am emotionally, mentally, and physically spent. Most days, I don't know where I find the strength to keep going, to face the mountain of challenges in front of us when all I want to do is stay in bed and hide under the covers. Love is my driving force. I will fight every day for Collin, and I know every day he will fight for me, for our boys.

God is blessing us with the strength and ability to continue when the road ahead is dark. We are praying for Collin to have more time, for the CAR-T to successfully eradicate all leukemia, and for Collin to eventually be healthy enough for a bone marrow transplant.

Day 497
May 13, 2022

I used to look forward to Fridays—the start of the weekend, a time for relaxation and fun. But now, Fridays fill me with dread. As the doctors' offices close for the weekend, I lose access to Collin's medical teams. Today, like most Fridays, I am anxious. Today is an important day, and I did not sleep at all last night. Collin is miserable, he is feverish, in extreme pain, and vomiting. I spent the night trying to keep him comfortable and stressing about all the unknowns of our situation.

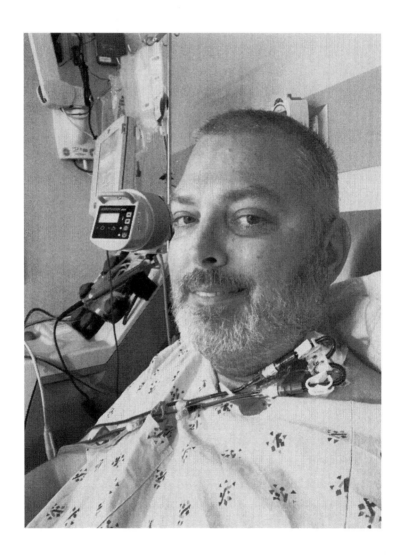

I dropped Collin off at Southeastern Memorial at 7:00 am for the T cell collection procedure. It is an outpatient procedure, but they would not allow me to stay with him. Instead, they instructed me to go home and informed me they would call when the procedure was finished. They estimated a return time of around 3:00 pm because the procedure is expected to take approximately eight hours from start to finish.

I emphasized the urgency of our situation to the nurse, explaining that I had to take him directly from Southeastern to Jackson Miller for hospital admission. She promised to give me at least a one-hour notice before he would be ready to be picked up, allowing me time to drive from our home, park, and make necessary arrangements.

As I drove home, I was a ball of nerves. My mind runs rampant with many terrible scenarios. I returned home and immersed myself in yard work—pulling weeds, pruning my flowers, fertilizing, and more. It was a futile attempt to quiet my racing thoughts and anxiety. While it felt good to be outside and move my body intentionally, the distraction provided little relief.

I called Collin every 30 minutes to check up on him, asking how he was feeling and for updates on his status. He sent me this picture, assuring me that his nurse was taking good care of him. In the photo, I could see the large IV they placed in his neck—he said it was uncomfortable, but he was happy the collection procedure was underway. He admitted he was feeling weak and had developed a migraine. He said, "I feel like I have been hit by a train, but I'm okay."

When this picture came through on my phone, I noticed how sick he looked. Our lives have become controlled by cancer, and my focus day in and day out is on doing everything I can in my power to keep Collin alive. As a result, I do not always notice how much his appearance has changed over the past year and a half. He is still my handsome husband with beautiful eyes and a smile that lights up the room, but the disease has completely changed him physically. And the moment I saw this picture, that fact hit me all at once, and I wept.

I allowed all of my emotions to pour out of me. I was mourning all that we have lost, all that cancer has stolen from us—our safety, our security, our freedom, our peace. I hate how unfair this is! It's not fair for our boys, it's not fair for me, and it's certainly not fair for Collin!

At 11:30 am, I received a call from Priscilla, the Nurse Navigator at Jackson Miller. Throughout this journey, she has become a friend and ally in overseeing Collin's care, and she was instrumental in helping to organize the events of today. I answered the phone, "Hi Priscilla," I noticed right away that she sounded a little frantic. "Kelci, there has been a mix-up with the insurance approval. Collin will now need to go to the Jackson Miller outpatient cancer clinic to receive his Besponsa and start the antibiotic for his mastoiditis. The insurance did not approve the Besponsa to be administered in the hospital." Confused, I replied. "He is at Southeastern Memorial getting his T cells collected now, but now

I am not supposed to take him straight to Jackson Miller Hospital to get admitted?" She clarified, "That is correct. As soon as he is done with his T cell collection at Southeastern, you need to take him straight to the Jackson Miller outpatient cancer clinic. They are expecting him. At the clinic, he will be administered Besponsa and the antibiotic for mastoiditis, and after that, you will take him across the street to Jackson Miller Hospital. Then they will proceed with hospital admission."

I was still confused. "I don't understand. I thought everything was good to go for us to go straight to the hospital?" She tried to be reassuring. "Everything is still good to go. The insurance approval came through for the Besponsa to be given at the outpatient clinic, not the hospital. So, you just need to get there as soon as Collin finishes at Southeastern Memorial. But Kelci, the outpatient clinic, closes at 5:00 pm, and it is closed on the weekend. If you don't get there before they close, he might not get his Besponsa treatment until Monday! What time is Collin supposed to be done at Southeastern?" I replied, "They said to expect around 3:00 pm." Priscilla instructed, "The drive from there to the clinic is about 30 minutes, so you should arrive at the clinic around 3:30 pm. That is cutting it close. Call me when you are on your way. I will make sure everything is ready for him, so they can start the Besponsa as soon as he arrives."

This conversation and new plan quadrupled my anxiety and stress level. But I confirmed I understood the new plan.

At 2:00 pm, I received a call from the nurse at Southeastern Memorial. She informed me the procedure was complete, and aside from not feeling well, he tolerated it fine. However, there was one problem: since Collin's platelet count (blood clotting factor) is very low, she could not safely remove the IV line from his neck. She explained she had started a platelet transfusion, and once the transfusion was complete in about an hour, she would attempt to remove the IV from his neck.

I reminded her of our time constraints, emphasizing that I had to get Collin to Jackson Miller at 3:30 pm for his immunotherapy and antibiotic treatments. I suggested leaving the IV line in place and having the medical team at Jackson Miller remove it; but she explained that for liability reasons, they could not do this. She promised she would work as fast as she could, and she would call me back in an hour.

After I got off the phone, I immediately called Priscilla and explained our new dilemma. She was worried, "Ugh! They need to understand that we do not have a minute to waste!" Pricilla told me she would make some calls to her contacts at Southeastern Memorial to persuade them to allow Collin to leave without removing the IV line in his neck.

Exactly at 3:00 pm, the nurse from Southeastern Memorial called me, just as she had promised. She informed me that Collin was still bleeding too much to safely remove the IV line, even with the platelet transfusion. Once again, I asked if they could leave it in place and let Jackson Miller remove it when it was safe to do so. She reiterated that it was not possible. Feeling desperate, I requested to speak to her charge nurse.

After a few minutes, the charge nurse came on the phone. I did not hold back my tears as I explained the dire nature of our situation. I stressed the urgency of getting Collin to the Jackson Miller outpatient cancer clinic by 5:00 pm before they closed for the weekend. In a final effort, I asked if I could sign a waiver, releasing Southeastern Memorial of all liability. However, once again, I was met with a firm refusal.

At this point, it was 3:30 pm. I couldn't sit at home anymore. I got in the car and started driving to Southeastern Memorial. My plan was to get Collin and sign him out AMA (against medical advice) with the IV line still in his neck. This was a matter of life and death, and every second counts!

As I was pulling out of my driveway, I called Priscilla to fill her in on my plan to break Collin out. Priscilla answered the phone, and before I could even get any words out, she said, "Hi Kelci, I was just picking up the phone to call you. I spoke to Dr. Raymond at Southeastern Memorial, and they are going to allow Collin to leave without taking the IV out. But you need to get him to the clinic as soon as possible! Call me when you are ten minutes away, and I will meet you at the entrance of the clinic, and we will get Collin's

Besponsa and antibiotic treatments started right away. The clinic closes at 5:00 pm, but I arranged for certain team members to stay late until Collin's treatment infusions are complete. The hospital has prepared his room, so as soon as he finishes at the clinic, you will take him across the street to the hospital, and they will take over from there."

Through tears of appreciation, I thanked Priscilla for being on our side and helping me fight for Collin. Throughout this journey, there have been countless moments where I have felt utterly alone, but this moment with Priscilla reminded me that I am not. There are hundreds, maybe even thousands, of people praying for Collin, for me, and for our boys, and those prayers are bringing miracles.

When I was ten minutes out from Southeastern Memorial, I called the nurse and asked if they could have Collin ready for me at the curbside, so we did not waste any time. She assured me she would have transport take him out to meet me. It was 4:05 pm when I pulled up, and I saw Collin in a wheelchair with the transport person standing behind him. He was still wearing the hospital gown they had him change into, the IV in his neck was oozing blood all over his gown.

I helped Collin into the car, and he told me his whole body was in pain, and he was certain he was about to vomit. My heart broke. He looked miserable. As I planted a gentle kiss on his cheek, I lowered his seat to its maximum recline. I handed him an emesis bag and told him how much I loved him, and I asked him to be brave for just a little longer. I got on the freeway quickly; I was worried about hitting Friday afternoon traffic, but miraculously, the traffic was light.

At 4:37 pm, I arrived at the entrance of the Jackson Miller outpatient cancer clinic. Priscilla was outside waiting for us with a wheelchair. I pulled up. Priscilla helped Collin out of the car and into the wheelchair. Then she instructed me to park while she checked him in.

Because the clinic was closing soon, there were plenty of empty parking spaces. Hurriedly, I parked the car and then grabbed my things to rush to Collin. But something stopped me. I paused and took a couple of deep breaths, then I offered a quiet prayer. It was a prayer of gratitude and a prayer for strength to endure whatever may come. As always, I pleaded for health and healing for Collin.

After my prayer, I rushed inside. It was a relief for me to see that Collin was already hooked up to the IV and the Besponsa infusion had started. I greeted his nurse and thanked her for replacing Collin's blood-soaked gown and the gauze dressing on the neck IV. Collin had his arm over his eyes to block the light from increasing the pain from his migraine. He also had an emesis bag in his hand. He looked miserable, and I wondered how much more suffering he could endure.

At 7:45 pm, the medication infusions were complete, and I drove Collin across the street to the hospital, where his room was ready and waiting for him. It is now 10:45 pm, and I am finally home. I will try to get

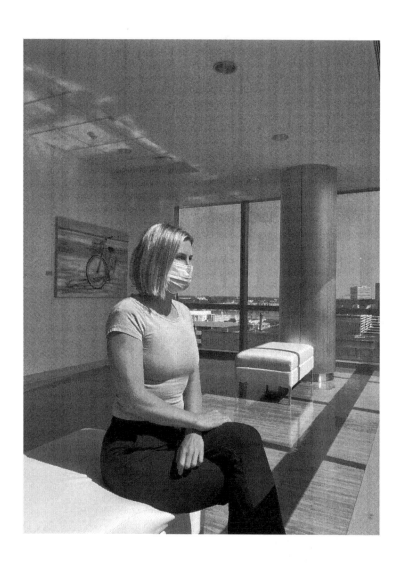

some sleep tonight, but I am doubtful I'll be successful. Nighttime seems to be when my anxiety peaks. I worry so much about Collin when I am not right by his side. Watching the person I love most in the world ravaged by disease is torture. It brings a misery that I would not wish upon my worst enemy.

Day 501
May 17, 2022

There is a spot just outside the doors to the oncology floor near the elevators where I often retreat to catch my breath, meditate, pray, and feel the warm sun. I sit in that spot now as I write this journal entry. The sunlight is streaming in through the windows, casting warm, golden rays that illuminate my otherwise sterile surroundings. Now and then, the familiar ding of the elevator doors breaks the silence, followed by the sound of footsteps as nurses and doctors hurry past, their swift movements a constant reminder of the urgency that permeates this place.

The last few days have been incredibly stressful. Last night, they could finally safely remove the IV line in his neck. But the leukemia in Collin's liver is causing him severe pain. His kidney function is deteriorating, so they had to hold off administering the chemotherapy over the weekend.

Thankfully, he could restart the chemotherapy last night. He has received multiple blood transfusions, but he just can't seem to keep his blood counts up. The IV antibiotics are helping to clear up the infected skull bone. As of now, he will not need to have another surgery to remove more bone. He is extremely weak and tired, but the immunotherapy and chemotherapy are slowly decreasing his leukemia blast numbers.

Five days ago, his leukemia blast count was 29%, and yesterday it was down to 18%, so we are moving in the right direction, albeit much slower than I would like. Pathology has not provided the numbers for today yet, but we are expecting them to be even lower.

Right now, his T cells are in the lab being transformed into little cancer killers. They will be ready for infusion the week of May 30th. In the meantime, he will continue to receive chemotherapy, and we are praying his body will be strong enough to endure a little longer so he can have a successful CAR-T cell transfer.

Day 505
May 21, 2022

Yesterday's scans did not bring the news we were hoping for. The leukemia is still hanging on strong in Collin's liver, despite everything we have thrown at it. The treatments are killing the leukemia in the blood, but not in the liver. His liver enzymes keep climbing, and his eyes are a bright yellow, taking me right back to February last year when he was in liver failure. He is suffering from swelling, confusion, and extreme fatigue. With the liver not functioning properly, toxins will continue to build up in his bloodstream.

He received his last dose of chemotherapy for this phase. As his case gets more complex, the oncology team is tirelessly brainstorming the best course of action. With approximately ten days until his CAR-T cells are ready for infusion, the countdown intensifies. Collin's body suffers from severe bruising and excessive bleeding because his platelet count is only 5,000 (the normal range is 150,000 to 450,000). His white blood cell count is zero, therefore, he has a very high risk of infection.

Despite these challenges, Collin is fortunate to have an exceptional team of doctors and nurses providing him with outstanding care, and they all love him. The team and Jackson Miller have become like family, and we are extremely grateful for their dedication and sacrifice to help heal those who are ill.

They are heroes, and you know who else are heroes? Blood donors. Collin has needed hundreds of blood products, each one saving his life. For many years, Collin himself was a dedicated blood donor, routinely giving his blood every couple of months to help others. Now, he is receiving the same life-saving gift he once freely gave.

Day 508
May 25, 2022

I feel like someone has punched me in the gut. This afternoon, Dr. Raymond delivered the most terrible news: Collin's T cells are not mutating into CAR-T cells. This is a devastating blow! CAR-T cell therapy is our only hope to get Collin well enough to bridge to a bone marrow transplant. But now, that hope is slipping away!

I asked Dr. Raymond how many times he had seen this happen. He said that it's a rare situation, occurring only about 10% of the time. However, he admitted he'd never had a patient in this circumstance before. He encouraged me not to give up; he said the lab has enough frozen T cells left over from Collin's original collection to try one more time, but there are no promises they will mutate into CAR-T cells on the second attempt.

If they mutate properly, June 18th is now the new estimated date the CAR-T cells will be ready. This pushes the CAR-T infusion date back at least three weeks! Because of his toxic liver levels, Collin is not coherent enough to understand what's happening. He's living on borrowed time. I am desperately clinging to the possibility of a miracle.

I reached out to everyone I know, asking for prayers. Prayers that his T cells will successfully mutate into CAR-T cells, and prayers that the leukemia will remain under control during this agonizing wait.

Right now, I'm feeling completely overwhelmed, and I cannot shake this sense of defeat that's settled in the pit of my stomach. My hands are shaking uncontrollably, and my heart is pounding so hard in my chest that it aches. It's like there's a weight pressing down on my body, making it hard to breathe. My head is spinning, and I'm having a hard time focusing on anything other than the overwhelming flood of emotions crashing over me.

When I returned home from the hospital, I got into the bath, submerging completely under water. There, I opened my mouth and screamed, a silent torrent of anguish, frustration, and fear unleashed. The water swallowed my cries, muting them into echoes that roared in my ears yet spared the boys from my pain. Screaming under the water allows me to express anger, frustration, sorrow, and fear without alarming them. In that moment, I let the water try to purge me of my torment, to wash away the layers of sorrow that clung to me. For a brief respite, I allowed myself to crumble, to drown in a private pity party.

Tomorrow is another day to fight. I will continue to search for the light in this suffocating darkness.

Day 510
May 27, 2022

I believe in miracles! Today, Collin's condition has shown marked improvement. This is not a coincidence! God is so good! Prayers are being answered, and Collin's liver levels are decreasing, removing the toxins that have built up in his blood. This improvement has allowed him to be more alert and coherent. He even got out of bed and did one lap around the oncology floor, and he didn't even need a walker. This is truly miraculous!

We continue to pray that his T cells will respond in the lab to genetic engineering and turn into CAR-T cells. I have seen the power of prayer and faith repeatedly; I know if it's God's will, it will be done.

Day 515
May 31, 2022

This morning, when I arrived at the hospital, Collin was sleeping peacefully. Not wanting to disturb him, I quietly set about organizing his bedside table, freshening up his water pitcher with ice water, tossing out any trash, and so forth. As I tidied up, I noticed two candy wrappers in the garbage, one from a king-size Reese's and the other from king-size Skittles.

Now, I know Collin is a grown man, and he can make his own choices, but given his fragile health, I highly discourage him from indulging in junk food like candy or soda. But sometimes, when I am not around, I know he sneaks it. I was curious about where those wrappers came from, and since Collin was asleep, I asked his nurse.

She recounted this hilarious story. After I left the hospital last night, Collin summoned the strength to make a late-night journey to the vending machine on the oncology floor. I didn't know there was a vending machine, but Collin sure found it. The twist? While he was off on his little snack quest, his nurse went into his room and found it empty. She panicked, scouring the area and rallying other nurses to join the search for him. She recounted, "We were all in a frenzy, fearing the worst, muttering, 'If we've lost Collin, Kelci is going to have our heads!'"

Just when they were about to call a "Code Yellow," which alerts hospital security that a patient is missing,

Collin strolled back around the corner, clutching Skittles in one hand and Reese's peanut butter cups in the other. His nurse was not amused. "Collin!" she scolded. "What were you thinking? You cannot just wander off like that, you're too weak and unsteady. It is dangerous!"

I could not help but laugh when she recounted the tale. And Collin? Well, once he woke up and I asked him about his little escapade, he sheepishly admitted to it. "Yeah," he confessed with a grin, "I got a bit of a talking-to. They even put an alarm on my bed now, so every time I try to make a break for it, they'll know."

Oh, Collin! Nobody can make me laugh like you do!

Day 518
June 3, 2022

We are still hanging out at the hospital, with no end in sight. Today, Collin's platelet count is 3,000. A normal platelet count is between 150,000 to 450,000. Therefore, a platelet count of 3,000 is critically low, putting him at high risk of internal bleeding and brain hemorrhage. Despite receiving daily platelet transfusions, his body just cannot seem to hold on to the platelets. The cumulative effect of a year and a half of chemotherapy has ravaged his bone marrow.

Collin has spent more days this year in the hospital than at home. He hates being in the hospital, and he is incredibly eager to go home, even if only for a few days. It is gut-wrenching to hear him ask the doctors every day if he can leave. However, with his platelet count so dangerously low, he is too unstable for discharge.

My love for him grows with each passing day. Sometimes he is snippy with me, and sometimes he says hurtful things, but I know it is because I am his safe space. The man is suffering, and yet he remains the most patient, patient. My soul hurts when he hurts. My heart breaks when he lashes out. But I understand. I understand it is not directed at me, but at the relentless pain he is forced to endure. In his agony, he clings to me as his anchor in this storm. I am grateful that I can be his anchor. I will do anything for him.

One thing that has helped me survive these past 518 days is finding a reason to smile every day. When the ground feels like it's crumbling beneath my feet, I grasp onto something—anything—to keep the light shining through the darkness.

Day 520
June 5, 2022

This photo popped up on my phone's photo memories today, and at first, it brought a huge smile to my face. I remember that magical day in the Cayman Islands, a day spent as a family doing what we love most: adventuring. But my smile quickly faded as the harsh reality of our lives slapped me in the face. We may never get to adventure like this again.

Every day, I plead with heaven that Collin can return to a healthy state. But today brought more bad news! Collin's leukemia blast cells were counted at 30%, he developed a fever, and all other leukemia markers were up. His leukemia is so aggressive, it can skyrocket within hours. Tomorrow, his team of doctors will have a meeting to determine which chemotherapy remains an option for him. Treatments for him are becoming more and more complex and complicated.

Approximately ten more days until we discover if the second attempt to mutate the T cells into life-saving CAR-T cells was successful. I am praying so hard for those CAR-T cells. We need them now more than ever.

Day 521
June 6, 2022

Waiting to hear if the T cells are progressing as needed in the lab has been agonizing. Patience is a virtue I have not acquired, and I am weary of waiting for updates from the transplant team at Southeastern Memorial. A bit of internet research led me to the telephone number of the lab in Southern California that is manufacturing the CAR-T cells. I called the lab directly and asked for an update. They informed me that the cells are still in the manufacturing phase. I apologized in advance, acknowledging that I would call frequently for updates, but the person I spoke to was incredibly understanding and assured me I could call anytime. I will call back tomorrow. In the meantime, I'll focus on cultivating that virtue of patience.

Day 523
June 8, 2022

I am terrified. Fear has settled heavily in my chest; it constricts my breath and sends shivers down my spine. I feel as if my entire body is vibrating with terror, every nerve ending alive with the intensity of our reality. I am so scared; Collin's illness is progressing rapidly.

His leukemia blast count has shot up to 42%. While his kidneys are holding up, his liver is taking a beating from those stubborn leukemic infiltrates. He did not need a red blood cell transfusion today, and his platelets are hanging on by a thread. Platelet transfusions seem futile; his body is devouring them faster than they can be replaced. Witnessing this and being helpless to change anything is torture.

This reality is so cruel. I want to scream at the universe, "Why is this happening? We never agreed to this!" But I know these thoughts make it almost impossible to hold on to hope. So, I am trying to remain positive. I am trying to focus on the things that are moving in the right direction. They seem to be few and far between, but I cling to them like a lifeline. All the while, I continue to pray for a miracle in the form of those CAR-T cells.

I made another call to the lab today, seeking an update. They told me the cells have finished their manufacturing phase and are now undergoing testing. This is great news! But we will not know for another agonizing five days if they have transformed into the cancer killers we desperately need them to be.

P.S. Collin is still my favorite to snuggle. He spent most of the day sleeping, so I spent the day snuggled up next to him in his hospital bed. Even though he is not very responsive because he is so sick, his presence is so calming. Wherever he is, is where I want to be.

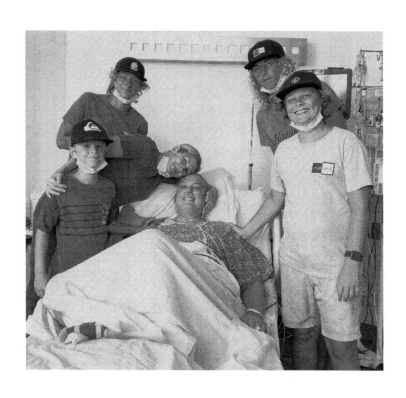

Day 525
June 10, 2022

Things are not looking good. The cancer isn't responding to the medications and therapies. Collin's latest scans show the leukemia is still throughout his liver, kidneys, spleen, and pancreas. The leukemia blast count in his blood is around 40%, and on top of it all, he's battling double pneumonia. His condition is getting worse by the day.

But there was a bright spot today. The boys had not seen Collin in over a week, so I asked my mom to bring them to the hospital for a visit. I worried Collin would not be awake or lucid when they came, but miraculously, when they arrived, Collin was awake and alert—the most he had been all week! He even found the strength to laugh and joke with them.

Collin's face always lights up when he gets to see the boys; I know this is one of the biggest reasons he hates being in the hospital. He misses his sons; he misses being a dad. Today, their visit with Collin was a tender mercy.

Day 526
June 11, 2022

Last night, a few hours after the boys came for their visit, I had an emotional breakdown. The realization hit me hard: the chances of life ever returning to the way it was before cancer robbed Collin of his health, robbed me of my husband, and robbed my children of their father, are slim. I'm not sure how to describe the physical pain of grief, but my whole body was throbbing with sorrow.

I crawled into the hospital bed and lay next to Collin, sobbing, my face buried in his back. Finding some comfort in listening to and feeling each breath he took. He was asleep, but he must have been woken by my distress. He whispered, "What's going on, Babe?" Most days, Collin does not understand what the doctors and I are discussing, both because he is so lethargic and not always alert and because he doesn't understand all the medical terminology. Thank goodness for my nursing background.

With a heavy heart, I explained to him that the leukemia was gaining strength and not responding to the treatments, and that he was running out of options and time. He cried and looked me dead in the eyes, saying, "I'm crying because you are sad, but I want you to know I'm going to be healed."

I wish I had as much faith as him! I have so much fear and doubt that sometimes it's hard to hold on to faith.

But this morning, he defied all odds AGAIN (I've lost count of how many times), and his leukemia blast count dropped to 19%! We are still in a very critical phase, but I heard from the lab today that Collin's CAR-T cells passed testing. Now we just have to wait a few more days for them to multiply!

Day 528
June 12, 2022

This morning, they transferred Collin from Jackson Miller Medical Institute to Southeastern Memorial Hospital. This is a big deal, as Southeastern Memorial now assumes the primary responsibility for Collin's treatment and care while we eagerly wait for his CAR-T cells to multiply and become ready for transplant. The anticipation is nerve-wracking, but we hope that these engineered cells will launch a targeted assault on the leukemia ravaging his body, affording us the precious window needed to pursue a bone marrow transplant.

Leaving behind the familiar faces at Jackson Miller feels like leaving a piece of our hearts; their team has become like family. They have seen us through the darkest of days. We know about their spouses and children, their hobbies, talents, and their likes and dislikes. It is so hard to leave all that behind; there were lots of tears and hugs as we left. But this transfer is a necessary step of progression in Collin's journey towards healing.

We still expect the CAR-T cell completion date to be June 18th, with the cells arriving at Southeastern on June 20th. We've got one more week, which seems like forever! I am so anxious; there are so many things that have to fall into place for this plan to work.

But we got some encouraging news today! Collin's leukemia blasts in the blood were down to 6% today! His pneumonia is improving, and his platelet count has increased to 11,000! This is the first time in four weeks that his platelet count has been over 10,000! Unfortunately, his liver is still showing signs of failure. The liver is failing because of the intense medications he is receiving and the leukemia that is still spreading throughout his liver.

We must take each day as it comes, putting forth a concerted effort to balance the emotions of hope and despair. Collin and I are dedicated to pressing forward, actively searching for the light, and acknowledging God's hand.

Day 533
June 18, 2022

The past few days at Southeastern Memorial Hospital have been challenging. Getting acquainted with all the new staff, doctors, nurses, and therapists is exhausting. We had such a good rapport with everyone at Jackson Miller, so it's hard not to compare every single person here with the ones we loved there. I know it's not fair, but it's the truth.

But the worst part is today's news: Collin's leukemia blast count is high again, now at 80%. This news took us by surprise. Normally, when his blast count gets this high, he feels very sick, with extreme pain, high fevers, and nausea. However, aside from being extremely weak and tired, he does not have any pain. I am so thankful for this tender mercy, but the grief I feel is overwhelming, it's almost unbearable.

He needs the CAR-T cells! Collin starts Day 1 of 3 days of preconditioning chemotherapy today to prepare his body to receive the CAR-T cells on Wednesday. This chemotherapy is designed to wipe out any remaining T cells he currently has, so the CAR-T cells can successfully take over and eliminate the cancer.

Also, his pneumonia is not improving, and it is getting harder and harder for Collin to breathe. He is requiring more and more supplemental oxygen. Despite extensive tests, including a bronchoscopy lavage performed yesterday, the doctors still have not been able to identify the exact cause of his ongoing lung issues. But the pulmonologist is now considering the possibility that his "pneumonia" may actually be bleeding. A result of lung damage from the chemotherapy, coupled with his extremely low platelets. This damage allows blood to seep into the airspace of his lungs, therefore interfering with his oxygen exchange. This is extremely dangerous and super concerning.

Tomorrow is Father's Day, and the emotions hitting me today are just indescribable. I keep trying to push away thoughts that this might be Collin's last Father's Day with us on this side of heaven. Yet, I cannot ignore our horrific reality. My soul is in turmoil, and I am caught in a confusing space between anguish that is sprinkled with gratitude.

This photo captures a moment of bliss and innocence as Collin and the boys laugh together in the hot tub at the club we belonged to for many years in California. We have spent hundreds of hours as a family at this club. Sometimes Collin would take the boys solo, giving me a much-needed "mommy break". This picture fills

me with an overwhelming sense of gratitude for the beautiful memories we have shared, but it also serves as a painful reminder of the life that has been ripped away from us, and the unfairness of our situation.

Life has a cruel way of throwing unexpected obstacles. While we may not be able to control the curveballs life throws at us, we can control how we respond to them. Today has been dark, and I know there will be more dark days ahead. One way I have learned to survive the darkness is to try daily to search for the light. Once I find a ray of light, I hold on to it like my life depends on it, because it does. I must live each day with purpose and intention. Because it is on the darkest nights that the stars shine the brightest.

Day 536
June 21, 2022

Today is our 19th wedding anniversary. Nineteen years ago today, I hit the husband jackpot when I said yes to the love of my life, the man of my dreams. Collin, our life has not unfolded exactly the way we envisioned, but through it all, you're the one I want by my side. There's no question, I would choose you a million times over.

I got a call at 3:00 am this morning; it was Collin's night nurse, informing me of a distressing situation. Collin was struggling to breathe and vomiting bright red blood. They transferred him from the oncology transplant unit to the ICU for closer monitoring. Though not on a ventilator, he is now on BiPAP, which is a type of breathing support machine that helps keep the airway open.

I got dressed right away and rushed to be by Collin's side. Today, as I sat by Collin's bedside, I reflected on our twenty-three years together, nineteen of those we've been married. We have had quite the adventure, with many twists and turns, highs and lows, but one thing has remained constant: our unwavering love and devotion to each other has never faltered. We have shared countless tears and belly laughs; we've experienced joys and sorrows, and through it all, our bond has grown stronger.

In this moment of crisis, as Collin battles to breathe and his body fights against unseen forces, I think of the promises we made to each other on our wedding day: to stand by each other in sickness and in health, for better or for worse. And today, as I gaze upon his frail body, surrounded by beeping machines and bustling medical staff, I feel so privileged to be the one who gets to support him through this hell. I know that is a strange thought, but I am grateful I can show up for him in a way that I know if the roles were reversed, he would show up for me.

I wish we were celebrating our 19th wedding anniversary on a romantic vacation on an exotic tropical island, but I cannot deny how grateful I am for every moment we've shared, the good and the bad. We have received incredible blessings. The truth remains: no matter what lies ahead; I am certain of one thing; because I get to call Collin mine, I am truly the luckiest woman in the world.

Day 537
June 22, 2022

4:00 am: I am home, asleep in our bed. I am awoken by my phone ringing. I sleep with my phone on my nightstand next to my bed with the ringer on loud just in case I get a call from the hospital. Groggily, I answer, my heart pounding with a mix of dread and urgency. It is the ICU doctor. His tone is serious as he delivers the devastating news. Collin is crashing, he is in a respiratory crisis and urgently needs to be placed on a ventilator.

"Mrs. Jager, do I have your permission to intubate your husband and put him on life support?" The doctor's voice breaks through the haze of shock, waking me up immediately.

"Yes," I reply, my voice trembling with emotion. "Please tell him I love him, and I'm on my way."

4:25 am: I am in the car, rushing to get to the hospital. The whole 30-minute drive, I am desperately praying for strength for Collin and strength for myself. I know it is going to be traumatizing to see him in this state, but we have been here before, and we got through it. We will get through it again.

5:05 am: As I step into Collin's ICU room, the sight before me is overwhelming. He lies there, pale and still, hooked up to a dozen different machines. Tubes and lines snake across his body, connecting him to various monitors and IV drips.

Doctors and nurses move with purpose around Collin's bedside, their expressions a mix of concentration and concern. I approach his bedside. I feel physically ill, like I am going to vomit. The air is thick with the scent of antiseptics, and angst. I reached out to touch his hand, and as tears streamed down my face, I whispered in his ear, "Collin, I am here," my voice cracking with the weight of unspoken fears. "I love you so much, and the boys love you so much. We are so proud of you. You're an amazing husband, always there for me, and a loving father who inspires our children. We couldn't be luckier. Your CAR-T cells are coming today, so please hang on a little longer. Please, Collin. Please, I need you to hang on just a little longer."

I was hoping for some sort of response from him, but I got nothing. Despite my knowing that he is receiving drugs that place him in a medically induced coma, I am desperately longing for a sign of acknowledgment-anything to assure me he could hear my words, my pleas, and feel my love. I held his hand and continued to whisper words of love and encouragement, praying that somehow, he would hear me and know that he was not alone.

7:00 am: The day shift nurse arrives. I am relieved; it is the same nurse who has been caring for Collin for the last two days. I asked her, "When is the CAR-T cell infusion scheduled to take place?" She explains she needs to coordinate with the oncology nurses, as they would come to his room and administer the cells.

8:15 am: Dr. Raymond enters the ICU room with his oncology team. He looked concerned as he walked over toward me. Then came the earth-shattering news: Collin can no longer receive the CAR-T cells as planned; the leukemia has surged to 96%, causing organ failure and shutting down his body. Devastated, my knees buckle, and I plead with Dr. Raymond to give him the CAR-T cells anyway, desperately clinging to the slim thread of hope that remains. If we wait any longer, I fear we might lose our chance altogether.

Dr. Raymond's response is crushing: "I'm sorry to say, I think we may have already missed our window of opportunity."

I continue to beg, "Please, just give him this one last chance. He has fought so hard; you must give it to him. Please, I am begging you!" Dr. Raymond somberly replied that he would consult with the rest of the hematology transplant team, and he would return in a few hours.

Feeling hopeless and defeated, I sobbed over my husband's unresponsive body. My friend Amie was there, offering emotional support as we clung to each other, pleading for heaven's mercy. I reach out to family and friends, begging for healing prayers on Collin's behalf.

11:45 am: Dr. Raymond returns. This time, he enters the room with a smile on his face. He tells me that Collin has slightly stabilized, and he and the other doctors on the hematology team believe Collin is now ready to receive the CAR-T cells thanks to the improvements he made in just a few hours! I am ecstatic! I awkwardly hug Dr. Raymond and offer my most sincere gratitude.

12:30 pm: Finally, after weeks of anxious anticipation, Collin received his CAR-T cells! Dr. Raymond cautioned me that there is no guarantee this is going to work and that we are still in for an exceptionally long, bumpy ride. With confidence, I looked him square in the eyes and said, "Collin is the 'Comeback Kid'. He is going to surprise you; he always does!"

Day 540
June 25, 2022

The CAR-T cells are working! However, Collin is experiencing many of the dangerous side effects of CAR-T cell therapy. The doctors expected these side effects; we knew going into the treatment that it came with many dangerous risks. One of the side effects of CAR-T is neurotoxicity. Collin is displaying signs and symptoms of neurotoxicity, but it is difficult to determine the extent since he is sedated.

He is on continuous 24/7 dialysis for acute kidney failure, but the injury seems to have hit its peak, and his kidney panel labs are trending down. His liver function tests also show that his liver is healing, which means the CAR-T cells are clearing the leukemia from his liver. He is still in critical condition, and we still have a long road ahead of us, but I am over the moon for any signs of progress.

The doctors tell me it's too early to predict which way Collin will go. He could get worse, or he could get better. But I know Collin, and he will beat this!

There is strength in numbers. I am in awe of the army that is behind us, and I draw strength from the outpouring of prayers and support. We have already seen so many miracles, and I believe there are many more to come.

Day 542
June 27, 2022

The Comeback Kid is back! Yesterday, the ICU team began weaning Collin off the ventilator, and today they removed the breathing tube, and he is completely off the sedation! He is alert and completely coherent! The neurotoxic side effects from the CAR-T cells are subsiding, and his leukemia blast count continues to drop daily. Dr. Raymond walked into his ICU room this morning and saw Collin sitting up in bed, alert and breathing on his own. Dr. Raymond's mouth dropped to the floor, and he said, "Wow, you're a sight for sore eyes! You, sir, are remarkable!"

God is so good! His grace has guided us through the darkest days, and now, as I witness Collin's miraculous recovery, I feel like I can take a deep breath. Of course, we have a long way to go, but I am soaking in every waking moment I have with Collin right now. Each breath he takes without the aid of machines, each word he speaks with clarity and coherence, feels like a precious gift. I am clinging to these moments, savoring

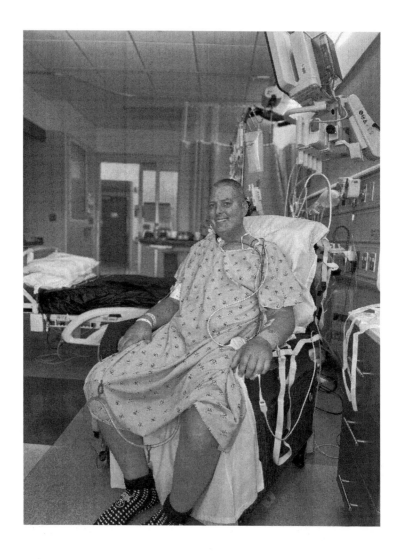

the simple joys of being by his side, holding his hand, and feeling the gentle reassurance of his presence.

Day 544
June 29, 2022

I stand all amazed! The abundance of miracles that God has given us in these past 7 days is truly astonishing. Just last week, I was bracing myself for the possibility of saying goodbye to my husband, and yet here he is today, sitting up in his chair, gracing me with his beautiful smile lighting up the room.

For over a year and a half, this incredible man beside me has endured unimaginable challenges, navigating through the depths of sorrow. Yet, amidst the darkness, he has remained steadfast, never once wavering in his faith, never once asking, "Why me?" He faces each challenge with a humble resolve that is inspiring. Every single day, he makes a conscious choice to show up—for himself, for me, and for our boys.

Though there are moments when the weight of his journey bears heavy upon him, when he mourns the life he had before cancer, he faces those emotions with courage and grace. He allows himself to feel the hurt, the pain, the despair, and then he rises, ready to fight once more.

Day 548
July 3, 2022

I've been struggling with how to express the whirlwind of emotions coursing through me adequately. Yesterday, we received crushing news: Collin's leukemia blast count has skyrocketed again, reaching a daunting 91%. The CAR-T cells went to work quickly, and Collin made rapid progress. This filled us with so much hope; witnessing Collin's miraculous recovery was what we had all prayed for!

But the progress has come to a screeching halt. Questions flood our minds: Have the CAR-T cells reached their peak, only to plateau? Is this the beginning of CAR-T failure? Or is this part of the process, and eventually the CAR-T will kill the leukemia again? The doctors do not have the answers to these questions, telling us not to lose hope, and that we have to take it day by day.

After we received this news and the oncology team left the room, I couldn't contain the tidal wave of hopelessness and despair that engulfed me. Tears streamed down my cheeks uncontrollably, and I knew I had to leave the room before I lost control. I didn't want to upset Collin further. I fled out of his room and ran down the ICU hallway, my sobs echoing against the sterile walls. Each step felt heavier than the last, burdened by the weight of uncertainty and fear. Eventually, I found an empty chair in the corner of the ICU family waiting room. Collapsing into the chair, I released a torrent of pain, fear, and anguish that had been building within me. It was a raw, primal outpouring of grief, the depths of which I have never experienced. The sound of my cries filled the room.

Suddenly, a stranger, a woman, approached me and silently took a seat in the chair beside me. Without a word, she offered a tender act of compassion: she gently placed her hand upon my trembling back. It was a simple gesture, yet it spoke volumes. At that moment, I felt so alone, and yet as I sat there, enveloped in the embrace of this stranger's kindness, I saw a tiny ray of light. I need these constant reminders that in the darkest of times, we are never truly alone. God is always by our side.

After a few minutes, I gathered my composure and returned to be with Collin. He was peacefully lying in bed, with his eyes closed. I sat down beside him and took his hand. Surprisingly calm, and with so much love in his eyes, he looked at me and said, "Kelci, everything is going to be okay. I am going to be healed. Please do not worry. I will get through this, and you will get through this." I questioned how he could be so sure. He replied, "Because I have seen the miracle. I had a vision, and I witnessed my body undergo a miraculous transformation, eliminating all disease. We need to hang on a little longer; the miracle is coming." His calm demeanor and his confidence in the words he spoke gave me some hope and peace.

But, I am not as confident as Collin that the miracle we are desperately praying for will be answered in the way we desire. I know God has a plan for Collin, for me, for our family. Whatever that plan may be, I know He will help us through. I also know that regardless of the outcome, the love and bond between Collin and me will remain unbreakable. That is the simple truth that I am holding onto. That is the truth that will give me the courage to keep pressing forward.

Day 551
July 6, 2022

Collin approached me with a request last night. He asked if I could arrange for Elders from our church to come to the hospital and offer him a blessing. It was a humbling experience as, within a few short hours, five devoted men came together at his bedside, ready to provide spiritual support. Their willingness to serve in this capacity moved us profoundly, and we are grateful for their ability to answer the call.

Before the blessing began, Collin updated the Elders on his current condition and prognosis. Despite the gravity of his situation, he spoke with unwavering confidence, expressing his belief that this trial was merely a bump in the road on his journey to healing. He spoke of his firm conviction that soon he would be relieved of this burden, through what he expected to be a miracle.

During the blessing, Collin received words of profound comfort and assurance. He was reassured of God's great love for him, and the purpose of this trial. He was reminded to remain patient. I already thought he was the world's most patient, patient. But apparently, he needs to be patient a little longer. I had hoped to hear words that would confirm Collin's expectation of healing, but unfortunately, those words were not spoken.

As for updates on Collin's condition, there has been little change in the past few days. Unfortunately, because of his extremely low white blood cell count, the pathologist cannot conduct a blast count to determine the extent of the leukemia. In the meantime, we continue to rely on supportive care, with a bone marrow biopsy scheduled for next week to provide a clearer diagnosis.

Despite the challenges we face, our hearts remain heavy but hopeful. We find solace in our faith and continue to pray fervently for additional miracles to come our way.

Day 556
July 11, 2022

"We just don't know where this is going yet." These are the words the doctors have said to us daily for the past week. Things have not progressed one way or another. Collin is still extremely sick; he is undergoing dialysis and requires constant blood transfusions. But, on the bright side, he's breathing on his own, and he is experiencing very little pain.

The doctors keep telling us to not lose hope, that even though the chances of survival are low, they are not impossible. And since Collin has been on the brink of death many other times and has always surprised us, we hope that he will make another miraculous recovery. He is bruised and battered from head to toe, and it would be an understatement to say that he is extremely exhausted. But he is alert and aware, and he makes me smile every single day.

Day 557
July 12, 2022

I am truly blessed to have such incredible support from the amazing women in my life, particularly my mother and Collin's mother. They've been taking turns flying in from the West Coast to lend a helping hand with the boys, the house, and everything in between. My mother left for California just one day before Collin's CAR-T cell stopped working after spending three weeks here. Without skipping a beat, Collin's mother, Kelli, immediately booked a flight to be by our side. My dear friend Shauna, from Washington State, is also here, lending a hand and offering loving support.

When Collin's condition is unstable, I refuse to leave him alone at the hospital. Kelli and I have formed a seamless tag team—I am with Collin during the day, and Kelli takes over the night shift, allowing me to go home and get a semblance of rest.

Today, Kelli arrived at the hospital unusually early, around 3:00 pm. I felt guilty leaving his side so early in the day. I wanted to stay with him, but I also desperately needed a reprieve. Reminding myself that Collin wouldn't be alone, knowing he would be in the loving care of his mother, I reluctantly decided to step away. It was a tough choice, but I knew it was necessary for my well-being. I told Kelli I would return early tomorrow morning.

Full of anxiety, I stepped outside the hospital doors, and immediately, the sight of the clear blue sky and the warmth of the sun on my skin offered a temporary escape. I forgot how good it feels to enjoy the simple joys of nature.

As I began driving home, an overwhelming urge to go to the beach washed over me. The ocean has always been my sanctuary, my favorite place to find peace. Typically, by mid-July, I would have already enjoyed countless beach days. However, cancer has consumed my life, and I can barely recall the last time I felt the sand beneath my feet and heard the soothing rhythm of the waves.

But today, the stars aligned, and I could make a trip to the beach happen. Without hesitation, I called Shauna and shared my desire. True to her supportive nature, she enthusiastically agreed, recognizing the significance of the opportunity. Promising to inform my sons of our spontaneous plan, Shauna also reached out to our other dear friend, Jessica, to join us.

I was at the beach within an hour, my toes buried in the warm sand, and the salty air engulfing my senses. With a surge of exhilaration, I charged into the warm summer sea, diving under the first crashing wave. At that moment, it felt as if all my worries were being swept away, replaced by a profound sense of vitality and liberation. It was as though the sea itself was mending my fractured soul.

Soon, Shauna and Jessica joined me in the ocean, and amidst laughter and playful splashes, I expressed gratitude for the euphoria washing over me. In their company, I felt a fleeting sense of innocence and joy, reminiscent of my carefree childhood days.

Yet, as we emerged from the water and settled onto the sand, immediately my world went dark again. Suddenly, reality zoomed in, flooding me with doubt, fear, and overwhelming despair. It was then, in the depths of my anguish, an undeniable truth resonated within my heart and soul—the realization that Collin's time on this earth was drawing to a close.

I started to weep, and Shauna and Jessica, sensing my distress, grew concerned. I tried to explain to them the message my soul was conveying. They were confused and questioned if the doctors had delivered dire news. I shook my head, explaining that while the doctors urged us not to lose hope, in this moment I knew without a doubt that the end was near. The admission of this truth is excruciating, and it is crushing my spirit to the core.

Chapter Ten

We Do Not Want to Say Goodbye

Day 558
July 13, 2022

Last night was brutal. After I revealed to Jessica and Shauna what I knew to be true in my heart, I put a mask on my face and pretended like everything was fine for the boys. I do not want to worry them; they have been through more heartbreak and trauma than any child should ever experience. I will do anything to protect their innocence for as long as possible.

It's been months since I've had a decent night's sleep, and after the epiphany on the beach, there was no chance of my nervous system settling down enough to allow rest. Instead, I lay in bed, consumed by anxiety and despair. Constantly refreshing Collin's lab results in the patient portal. Hoping for some sort of evidence to disprove my beliefs. But with each update, the numbers paint a bleaker picture. His vital organs are failing, his cancer markers are off the charts, and I know this is CAR-T failure. Collin has been on the brink of death many times before, but this time is different. The certainty of this knowledge is unbearable. It's too much for me to handle. I cannot comprehend any way that Collin will survive this, and I don't know how I will survive without him.

Being alone at home only amplifies the torture of my dark thoughts. At 3:30 am, I couldn't take it anymore. I got into my car and drove to the hospital. I texted Collin's mom, Kelli, informing her I was on my way. The 30-minute drive felt like an eternity. The closer I got, the more I cried.

When I reached the hospital, Kelli emerged through the entrance doors. She looked worn out and relieved by my presence. I enveloped her in a hug, unable to hold back the torrent of emotions. "Kelli," I whispered, "the end is near. Collin's labs confirm our worst fears. It's time to prepare ourselves for the unthinkable." Her tears mirrored mine as she uttered words of hope, saying she was following the doctors' instructions to not give up hope. I managed to put on a half-hearted smile, nodding in understanding, though in my heart I knew the truth.

I hurried up the elevator to Collin's bedside. He was asleep and appeared peaceful. Tenderly, I placed a gentle kiss on his lips and whispered, "I love you, Collin." Taking a seat beside him, and although he remained asleep, I clasped his hand, seeking solace in his presence.

Unable to contain the flood of emotions, I buried my face in the side of his bed and sobbed. Candice, his nurse, noticed my distress and compassionately approached me, placing her hand on my shoulder and offering a box of tissues. "Kelci, can I get you anything?"

she asked, her concern palpable. I shook my head, declining her offer. "Candice, I know." My voice thick with emotion. She gently probed further, "Know what?" I replied, my voice breaking, "I know the end is near." The weight of this truth hung heavy in the air. Her response was a silent acknowledgment. A single tear streamed down her cheek. "Have the doctors told you this?" she inquired softly. I shook my head, then buried my face once more into the rumpled sheets of the bed and continued sobbing.

I couldn't be sure if Collin had heard our conversation, as he appeared peacefully undisturbed. Hours passed, and I sat there watching the rise and fall of his chest, wondering how much longer he would be permitted to stay with us on this side of heaven.

I watched as the sun slowly rose over the horizon. I felt frustrated as the world continued to spin in normalcy for everyone else, but for me, it was coming to a shocking halt. As sunlight flooded the room, Collin began to stir. His eyelids fluttered open. Meeting my gaze, he gave my hand a gentle squeeze and blew me an air kiss. I could tell he was getting weaker, but he managed to whisper, "I love you, Babe."

My heart swelled with love and sorrow, knowing that each moment with him was precious and fleeting. "Good morning, my Love," I replied, my voice catching in my throat as I struggled to hold back tears. He closed his eyes and went back to sleep.

At approximately 8:15 am, the oncology team entered the room, their demeanor solemn, their steps measured with a heaviness that mirrored the weight of the news they carried. Tears already streaming down my face, I braced myself for the inevitable as their eyes met mine with a silent expression of pity.

Dr. Raymond approached Collin's bedside, gently shaking his leg to wake him from his slumber. "Mr. Jager, Mr. Jager, it's Dr. Raymond. Can you wake up for me?" Collin's eyes fluttered open slowly, and Dr. Raymond inquired about how he was feeling. Collin responded with a faint smile and a thumbs-up before closing his eyes once again and drifting back to sleep.

Dr. Raymond turned his focus to me, and I braced myself for confirmation of my worst fears. "Mrs. Jager," he began, his voice heavy with sorrow, "as you know, we've been closely monitoring the effects of the CAR-T cell therapy. When your husband received them, he was in critical condition, and we were uncertain of the outcome—whether they would exacerbate his illness or offer a chance at recovery. We were encouraged when they initially showed signs of effectiveness, aiding in his improvement."

I listened intently, my heart sinking with each word, as Dr. Raymond continued, "Unfortunately, the CAR-T cells are no longer working the way we had hoped. We are witnessing CAR-T cell failure." His words hung in the air. "I am deeply sorry, Mrs. Jager, but there is nothing more that we can do."

The room seemed to spin as his words sank in, the reality of our situation hitting me with a force I couldn't comprehend or prepare for. Despair washed over me as I struggled to process the finality of his pronouncement. In that moment, all hope was extinguished, leaving behind only the crushing weight of grief and the unbearable anguish of knowing that there was nothing left to do but to say goodbye.

Despite the overwhelming emotions coursing through me, somehow, I managed to maintain my composure and address the medical team with clarity. "He's going to want to go home. How much time does he have left?" I asked, my voice steady despite the turmoil within me. Dr. Raymond replied, "A few days at most." I reemphasized my request, "Please do whatever you can to get him home, as soon as possible."

Turning to Collin, I tenderly placed my hand on his face, "Collin, can you wake up?" I whispered, "The doctors need to talk to you." His eyes opened, and I could sense that he hadn't been entirely asleep, that he had heard our conversation.

As Dr. Raymond delivered the devastating news once more, Collin's expression remained stoic. Meeting my gaze, he uttered these simple yet poignant words, "I want to go home." My heart ached at the quiet resolve in his voice, and I promised him without hesitation that I would ensure his wish was granted.

The doctors left the room, and I immediately called Kelli. I told her what the doctors had confirmed and asked her to bring the boys to the hospital. Then I sat with Collin, and I asked him if he was scared. It was evident that his strength was waning with each passing moment. His words were becoming slurred, and his motor functions were diminishing. With his eyes closed, his voice was barely audible. "I am not scared," he whispered. "I wish I could stay. Because I don't want to leave you. I don't want to leave the boys. But I am not scared."

His admission was both comforting and heartbreaking. This is not fair! Why does he have to leave us? How could it be that the miracle we have desperately prayed for has not come to pass? We have faith. We have patience. None of this makes any sense!

Within the hour, the boys arrived, accompanied by Kelli and Shauna. As they entered the room, their young faces were etched with sorrow, and tears cascaded down their cheeks. Each of them walked in with their heads hung low, their pain palpable. Collin's eyes brightened as they entered, a fleeting attempt to muster strength for their sake. With a gentle embrace, he welcomed them, his voice tender and reassuring.

I could tell he was trying to be brave for them. Despite his pain, he found the strength to comfort his boys. He held them close, whispering words of reassurance, promising them that everything would be okay. That they would be okay. And though he will no longer be visible to them, he assured them that he would always be near, watching over them with unwavering love and guidance. My heart shattered into a million pieces as I witnessed this—the juxtaposition of my husband bravely comforting his sons while facing his mortality.

The room was heavy with emotion, as if each breath carried the weight of our collective grief. Saying goodbye to Collin is not just parting with a husband and father; it feels like we are losing the very heart of our family. Our children remained by Collin's side, taking turns sitting next to him and holding his hand. Sometimes they spoke to him, but mostly they sat in silence, grappling with the enormity of the situation.

Meanwhile, I updated our family members via text messages, conveying the heartbreaking news of Collin's condition. It felt surreal and impersonal to deliver such devastating news through a group text, but I lacked the emotional bandwidth to make individual phone calls. Instead, I instructed them to call my cell phone, and I would place it on speakerphone next to Collin so they could speak to him and say their goodbyes.

One by one, each of Collin's four siblings, my parents, and my siblings called, their voices filled with love and sorrow as they said their goodbyes. Despite his declining ability to talk, Collin remained cognitively present, listened intently, and tried to respond as best he could, managing to laugh, joke, and offer words of comfort—a testament to the kind of compassionate human he is, even in his final moments.

Eventually, I asked Shauna to take the boys home. It was a difficult decision, but I felt it was important for them to be surrounded by the familiar comforts of home during this tumultuous time, and Shauna's presence would also ensure that someone was there when the hospice bed and supplies were delivered.

The scene at the hospital felt surreal as hospital workers approached me with questions and decisions to be made, thrusting papers for me to sign. Amidst the chaos, I spoke with the palliative care doctor, hospice nurse, and social worker, with each conversation getting more and more unbearable.

As the medical team outlined the steps ahead, ensuring Collin's final moments would be as peaceful as possible, I felt a sense of resignation settle over me. This was our new reality—a reality filled with pain and sorrow, with no silver lining in sight.

Kelli and I remained at the hospital until the paramedics arrived to transport Collin home via ambulance. Finally, at 8:45 pm, they arrived, and as one paramedic handed me more papers to sign, the other asked a question that caught me off guard. "Where do you want us to transport him if he passes in the ambulance?" he asked.

Stunned by the question, I stuttered, "I don't know. Where else would you take him?" The paramedic explained that some people prefer to be taken directly to the mortuary to avoid the additional costs of transporting the body to the morgue. His words left me reeling. "I don't have a mortuary," I replied, feeling overwhelmed by the sudden realization of all the decisions that lay ahead. "I haven't even considered any of this. But I promised my husband I would get him home, so that's where we're going."

I climbed into the back of the ambulance; with Collin strapped into the gurney in front of me. One paramedic drove while the other sat with me in the back. It was a painful 30-minute drive to our home, the bumps in the road causing Collin to grimace with each jolt. With my hand resting on his, I silently prayed for his safe arrival home. He wanted to be there, surrounded by the familiar comforts of our family and the warmth of our home, and I prayed fervently for that blessing to be granted.

Finally, we arrived at our home. They wheeled the gurney through the front door, and there, waiting for us, were the boys, Shauna, and our Bishop, our spiritual leader akin to a pastor. The air was heavy with emotion as we gathered in the living room.

In the center of the room, amidst the rearranged furniture, was the hospice bed. Shauna, Ian, and Lucah had cleared the space, moving the furniture aside to make room. It was important to me that Collin be in the heart of our home, where he could feel surrounded by the love and warmth of our family. Tucking him away in our bedroom didn't feel right; this was not what he would want. And so, there in the living room, surrounded by those he loved most, Collin in his final moments, was at the center of our world, both literally and figuratively.

Day 559
July 14, 2022

It's midnight, and I am sitting on the couch beside Collin, my heart heavy with anticipation and uncertainty. With every breath he takes, I wonder if it will be his last. I scrutinize every subtle movement for any sign of discomfort or distress. The doctors told us yesterday that he had a few days left at most. But since he is no longer receiving any supportive measures, I don't think he is going to make it through the day.

Honestly, I have conflicting emotions. On one hand, I am praying for an end to his suffering, for his journey to come to a peaceful close quickly. But on the other hand, the thought of him being gone is agonizing. It feels like I am living in a nightmare. It's almost impossible to comprehend.

Shauna sits beside me on the couch, reading a book. She's encouraged me to try to get some sleep, promising to keep a vigilant watch over Collin and wake me if he needs me. She'll be leaving for the airport at 6:00 am to catch her flight home, but she insists she can stay awake and read her book and then she will sleep on the plane. However, my emotions are too raw, and I don't think I can sleep.

Across the room, Maddox and Elijah are curled up asleep on the other couches; their innocent slumber is a stark contrast to the somber atmosphere that surrounds us. I gave them the option to sleep here in the living room next to their dad, or their beds. Ian,

Lucah, and Kelli have chosen to sleep in their rooms, but I've promised to wake them if it seems that Collin's time is drawing near.

I guess I will try to rest my eyes now, maybe I can get a little nap.

4:00 am: I am the only one awake; the house is quiet. I did get a few 20-minute cat naps here and there. I am still on the couch next to Collin's hospice bed; I listen to every breath he takes. They are more labored now than just a few hours ago. Occasionally he calls out to me, I rush to his side and reassure him, "I'm here and you are safe". He tries to utter a response, but his slurred words and weakness make it difficult for me to understand what he is trying to communicate.

6:00 am: Shauna just left. Saying goodbye was difficult. She felt bad for leaving me in such a dire time. Her presence has been so comforting these past few days, and she has been so helpful. Her visit was the perfect timing; I know it was divinely orchestrated.

6:10 am: I crawl into the hospice bed beside Collin, seeking solace. I snuggle up close, feeling the weight of the moment pressing down on me. With a whisper, I ask him to make me a promise. I ask if he will promise to visit me after he's gone and if he will visit me often. I ask for a clear sign, something unmistakable that will reassure me of his presence. I give specific instructions, "Make it obvious, so I will have no doubt it's you. I don't know what that sign will be," I confess, "but you will know what to do. Can you promise me this?" He ever so slightly moves his head, a silent but unmistakable yes. A faint sound escapes his lips, confirming his promise.

I thank him for this assurance. Then, I make my promises to him. I promise the boys and I will find a way to be okay, and that his legacy will live on through us. With conviction, I vow that his death won't be the end of me and that I will continue living fully, showing our boys that life is still worth embracing, even when heartbroken.

As I make these promises, I worry I am promising the impossible. I am not sure how I will ever be able to keep them. Yet, deep in my soul, I know he needs to hear these promises from me. I think I needed to hear them too.

8:00 am: The morning light filters through the windows, casting a gentle glow across the room. The boys begin to stir, eager to spend these last precious moments with their dad. As the day progresses, the familiar sounds of laughter and conversation fill the air. The boys play Collin's favorite movies on the TV in the background. Comedy and action are his genres of choice, and the boys sit next to him as they watch his favorites. He can't open his eyes, but his sons are there for him, offering comfort in his final hours.

12:00 pm: My phone keeps buzzing incessantly with calls and text messages, and honestly, I can't bear to face them. I know they are all messages of love and support, but it's too much right now. I turned my phone off and stashed it away in a drawer of my nightstand.

There is so much kindness coming our way, and I appreciate it all. The kitchen counter is filled with containers and packages of food. I think the boys are eating, but I can't. The thought of eating makes me feel queasy. My stomach feels tied up in knots.

1:00 pm: Despite my efforts to stay strong for Collin and our boys, I've had multiple breakdowns. Each time I retreat to my bedroom alone and fall to my knees, overwhelmed by sorrow, my body shakes as I sob. My soul is utterly broken, my spirit is crushed. The pain of losing Collin is suffocating. The anguish feels as if it is physically tearing me apart from the inside out. My heart is being ripped apart. The pain is too intense for me to bear.

3:30 pm: I hate this! I'm struggling to find the words to express the depths of my devastation. Tears have poured from my eyes endlessly, and just when I think I've cried all I can, more come, as if from an infinite well of sorrow. My head is pounding, and my stomach feels like it's being ripped to shreds. Yet, amidst this agony, there's an inexplicable sense of peace and gratitude that also envelops me. It's a paradoxical mix of emotions that defies logic, the worst day of my life, shattered beyond repair, yet somehow, I can see light.

In this darkest moment, I can't deny the tender mercies and miracles that have graced our lives over the past 559 days. I can see so clearly that God is in the details. Collin's life was prolonged numerous times. Even though the CAR-T cell therapy did not produce the results we hoped and prayed for, it allowed him more time. He stabilized and came back to us for a short time. I thought he was going to die in that ICU bed when they intubated and sedated him. I thought I was never again going to hear him say "I love you." But I did! He was able to see our boys and tell them his wishes and desires; he was able to tell them how much he loved them and how proud he is of each of them.

Collin hated being in the hospital, he never complained but frequently expressed his desire to go home. Once he made the decision yesterday to go home, the team worked fast to make it happen. And now he is home with us, just as he desired. These are all beautiful miracles that I can't negate because we aren't getting the one miracle that we desperately prayed for.

5:00 pm: Collin's breathing is very irregular. It's very shallow, and he has long pauses between breaths. He is no longer responsive to any sort of stimulus. I crawled into bed with him, snuggled against his body. I notice his body temperature has dropped. I place my hand on his face and reassure him again and again that it's okay for him to say goodbye. I called the boys, and his mother to gather around. I offered a prayer, asking God to grant Collin comfort and peace, I pleaded with Him to welcome Collin back into His presence.

5:22 pm: My gorgeous husband, Collin Cal Jager, peacefully takes his last breath and transitions from this life into the next.

Chapter Eleven

Death Is Not The End

Day 559
July 14, 2022

6:00 pm: I haven't moved from my spot beside Collin's body. It's astounding how I can physically see the shift in its appearance now that his spirit has departed. His body, once vibrant with life, now appears as nothing more than an empty shell.

Before this moment, I assumed I would want to call the mortuary immediately after his passing. I imagined it would feel grim or unsettling to keep his body here. But now, I feel no sense of urgency. I'm not yet ready to part with him, not ready to have them take his body away.

Suddenly, I feel an urgent need to escape the confines of the house. The walls of the hospital have suffocated me for so long, that I yearn for the freshness of the outdoors. Making my way to the lanai, I start watering my plants. I feel a mix of devastation and peace as I reflect on what just happened. My mind cannot comprehend how watching Collin take his last breath was the most tragic event of my life, yet it was also peaceful and sacred.

As I try to sort this out in my mind, I find myself speaking aloud to Collin as if he's standing right beside me. His unique ability to calm me is palpable, even in his absence. The warmth of his presence surrounds me, filling me with a sense of familiarity and comfort.

A gentle breeze brushes against my skin, and I'm reminded of the blessing pronounced upon me by our Bishop just last night: "You will be blessed with moments when you can feel Collin in the air." And in that instant, I'm certain that he's here with me.

"Collin, are you here?" I speak the words aloud, longing for a sign of his presence. And at that precise moment, my phone vibrates in my pocket—a single, quick buzz. It's him, I'm sure of it.

Retrieving my phone, I realize it's a lightning strike notification from the lighting app I have installed. A smile tugs at the corners of my lips as I recall Collin's promise to visit me often and to leave me unmistakable signs. "Babe, your sign is brilliant," I say aloud, acknowledging his presence with gratitude. And as if in response, my phone buzzes again with another lightning notification, reaffirming his presence.

7:30 pm: Word spread quickly yesterday, among our neighbors that Collin was coming home on hospice care. They wasted no time in rallying together to support us. Without hesitation, they sprang into action, organizing a candlelight vigil to honor Collin. As they shared their plans with me, expressing their desire to gather outside our home at 7:30 pm, their outpouring of love and support overwhelmed me. Since Collin has now passed, I texted a neighbor and explained our need for privacy. I informed her we would observe the vigil from the sanctity of our home, watching from the windows.

My alarm chimes, breaking the silence. It's 7:30 pm. I call our sons downstairs, and their hurried footsteps echo as they race to join me. We approach the windows, and I am stunned to see a crowd of over a hundred people gathered outside on the sidewalk in front of our home. My heart swells with a whirlwind of emotions as I take in this overwhelming and unexpected outpouring of support and love.

Suddenly, I feel an impulse to honor Collin's spirit of courage and compassion. I turn to our children and declare, "If Dad were here, he would go outside." My voice wavered with emotion, "I am going to go out there. Who wants to come with me?"

My revelation takes Kelli aback. "You are going outside? Are you going like that?" she asks, her concern evident in her voice as she gestures towards my disheveled appearance. I chuckle at her question, aware of my unkempt hair, weary eyes, puffy face, and the fact that I haven't changed out of my pajamas.

With a sheepish grin, I nod. "Yep, I'm going just like this. Does anybody want to come with me?" I ask, fully expecting everyone to decline the invitation. In unison, they shake their heads, no, but determination is welling up within me. "Okay, well, I'm going," I announce, and with unwavering resolve, I make my way towards the front door.

Just as I begin to turn the doorknob, Kelli's voice stops me. "Wait, I'm coming with you." Together, arm in arm, we stepped out the door and down the driveway, united in our shared sorrow and fortified by our collective strength.

As we emerge, the crowd falls quiet, their murmurs fading into an uneasy silence. They hadn't expected us to join them, and their reaction was one of surprise and uncertainty. They are unsure of what to do next. In this awkward moment, I feel a surge of vulnerability wash over me. The weight of their collective gaze feels heavy, and I wonder if we have made a mistake in stepping outside. But as I look around at the faces in the crowd, I see only empathy and compassion reflected at us.

Slowly, the spell breaks, and one by one, individuals approach us. I feel the weight of their concern wash over me with each hug, each whispered word, offering love to my broken soul.

It doesn't take long for me to notice the sky; it is ablaze with lightning all around us. The most beautiful and awe-inspiring spectacle of lightning I have ever seen is happening right now. A 360-degree panorama of lights illuminating the distant horizon. As the flashes of light dance across the sky, everyone gathered can't help but marvel at the spectacle. Some joke that it's Collin putting on a show for us. "There is no way he would miss his vigil," I say with a smile, acknowledging the significance of the moment.

But deep down, I know there's more to it than mere coincidence. It is Collin! As I marvel at the brilliance of the lightning, a neighbor approaches me, excitement clear in her voice. "Kelci, I have to show you this," she says, gesturing towards her phone. With a sense of wonder, I glance at the weather radar displayed on the screen. A ring of severe storms encircles our area, yet right where we stand, the sky remains miraculously clear.

"It's as if we have angels surrounding us," she remarks, her words resonate deeply within me. I find so much comfort in the fact that Collin's presence is undeniable. The words, "Visit me often, and make it obvious," echo in my mind. He has indeed made it obvious. He is here, his love transcending every boundary—even death— reminding me that death is not the end and his spirit still exists.

July 15, 2022

The sun rose today, as it always does, casting its golden hues across the world, but my world is dark. For 559 days, I stood by Collin's side as he fought leukemia, but now his battle is over, and mine has just begun. This reality sinks in with brutal clarity. The thought of continuing life without him by my side is insurmountable, a burden too heavy to bear. Yet here I am, forced to confront it head-on.

I had hoped to spend today just sitting with my grief, catching my breath amidst the storm of emotions raging within me. But the world, unyielding in its demands, refuses to grant me even a small reprieve. There is a never-ending barrage of tasks and decisions that demand my immediate attention. Funeral arrangements, legal matters, financial affairs, business dealings—each clamor for resolution, threatening to engulf me. It's a harsh reminder that life keeps moving forward for everyone else, while ours stands still, shattered, and forever changed. I feel suffocated—suffocated by my grief, suffocated by expectations placed on me, suffocated by the world. I'm gasping for air.

There are so many chattering voices, though well-intentioned, only add to the noise already swirling in my head. I want nothing more than to run away, to hide from the overwhelming weight of it all. So, I'm making a deliberate choice—I'm shutting out the world. I don't care what others may say or think, my priority is clear: to cocoon my boys in a bubble of love and safety. Nothing else matters. Everyone else, and everything else, can wait.

July 16, 2022

I cried more than I slept last night. With my face buried into my pillow, I sobbed silently, not wanting to disturb Maddox, who slept peacefully beside me. During Collin's hospital stays, Maddox and Elijah started taking turns sharing my bed. It wasn't planned; it just happened. At first, it was out of necessity to ease their anxiety and fears. But over time, it became more than that. It became a comforting routine for all of us.

As the morning progressed, one by one, the boys emerged from their rooms, and the weight of grief hung heavy in the air. We all needed a break, a reprieve from the raw emotions swirling within us. So, I asked, "Who wants to go to the beach?" The excitement in their voices was palpable, as each child eagerly declared their desire to go. And just like that, we packed up the surfboards and headed to our happy place.

Our children have always been drawn to the water; they are like fish. I've often teased that they came out of the womb swimming. As we stepped onto the sandy shore, the familiar sights and sounds of the beach stirred a whirlwind of emotions within me. The gentle roar of the waves crashing against the shore, the salty tang of the sea breeze, and the warmth of the sun on my skin—all served as poignant reminders of happier times.

We've always lived by the beach, so we've spent countless days here. And all at once, vivid memories fill my mind; I see the image of Collin pushing our sons into the waves on their surfboards. I hear infectious laughter as he chased the boys along the shoreline, their joyous shouts mingling with the sound of the sea. I remembered the way Collin would glance at me to ensure I approved of the level of intensity he played with them. A silent understanding passed between us as we reveled in the joy of parenthood together.

These memories are so vibrant that I half-expect him to run up from behind, playfully wrapping me in a loving bear hug. Life was so grand with Collin; his presence filled our days with endless love, boundless joy, and a sense of adventure that enriched every moment we shared as a family.

And while these memories bring me an abundance of joy, they also come with debilitating heartbreak. A reminder of what once was that will never be again. At that moment, doubt crept in, and I questioned whether coming to the beach had been a huge mistake. The pain of his absence is paralyzing.

But then, as I watched our precious sons eagerly darting towards the water, their laughter ringing out like music, I knew that coming here had been the right choice. Despite the bittersweet ache in my heart, being here with our beautiful boys, surrounded by the vastness of the ocean, filled me with a sense of peace and connection. And I knew that there was hope for our family. I knew together we would figure out how to do this life, with Collin guiding us from the other side.

July 18, 2022

Today, I am confronting a profound truth that cuts deep—I am a 43-year-old widow. Writing that word feels excruciating, as if I'm admitting defeat. It's like bearing a scarlet letter, the weight of it heavy enough to crush my chest.

In this sacred space of my journal, I can speak freely, unburdening my heart without fear of judgment or misunderstanding. As I sit here grappling with the absence of my dear Collin, my heart aches with a pain I never imagined possible—a pain that feels as though it will never fade. How do I navigate this new path without him by my side? The uncertainty fills me with panic and desperation.

But I made a promise to Collin that I will not allow myself to be consumed by despair. Therefore, I must hold on to the belief that somehow, I'll find my way. No doubt, there will be moments when I stumble, and I will fall. But I must believe I have the strength to pick myself up and keep moving forward.

And by the grace of God, our family will not only survive but also thrive.

July 20, 2022

Today, the boys and I shared a heartfelt conversation about their dad. We reminisced about Collin's remarkable ability to forgive quickly and completely, his embodiment of loyalty, kindness, and selflessness, always looking for ways to serve others. Collin's love was fierce and unwavering, a guiding light for us all.

As we honored these cherished qualities of their father, we collectively vowed to embody his legacy. Like Collin, we pledged to contribute to a better world, spreading kindness and love in our daily lives.

During our conversation, we felt Collin's presence so keenly, as if he were right beside us. We recalled the promises he made to each of our children on his deathbed—that he would always be near, watching over them with unwavering love and guidance.

Amidst all the uncertainty swirling around us, there's one thing I know for sure: death is not the end. Collin

lives on; his spirit may no longer be in his body, but he exists. His courage, strength, faith, dedication, and love for his family continue to uplift and inspire, touching the lives of many.

July 22, 2022

This evening, we gathered on the beach near our home for a deeply meaningful ceremony: a Celebration of Life Paddle Out in honor of Collin. A paddle-out ceremony is a traditional ritual in surfing culture where friends and family remember and honor a loved one who has passed away. It involves paddling out beyond the ocean waves, forming a circle, and sharing memories and reflections before releasing flowers into the sea as a final farewell.

As we gathered on the beach, the waves serving as our backdrop, we shared memories and stories of Collin. Laughter mingled with tears as we recounted his infectious smile, warmth, humor, and the love he brought into our lives. Then, with heavy hearts, we grabbed our boards and embarked on one last paddle out in his honor. It was a symbolic gesture, a final tribute to Collin's love for the ocean and his passion for surfing. Forming a circle in the water, I sat on Collin's surfboard and said a few words. We released our flowers and then splashed and hollered.

Amidst the waves and the salty air, I felt a whirlwind of emotions. Grief weighed heavily on my soul, yet there was also a sense of joy and unity in honoring Collin's memory together.

After bidding farewell to Collin, we remained in the water, riding the waves and sharing laughter in his honor. As I made my way back to shore, Collin's surfboard under my arm, I couldn't help but speak to him aloud. "Babe, you always have known how to bring people together. You would have loved this."

And in that moment, as if on cue, a massive lightning bolt branched off in the distant horizon, a sign from Collin himself. As if to say, "Babe, I am here."

July 23, 2022

Collin's memorial service was this morning. From the moment I woke up, the whole scene in front of me felt surreal. As I drove to the chapel, I felt a sense of determination and confidence in my ability to navigate through the service. But as soon as I entered the church building and saw videos of Collin and our family playing on the TV screen, I lost all composure.

At that moment, it became abundantly clear that Collin wasn't coming home. Despite knowing this logically, my mind has struggled to comprehend it. It's as if my mind still holds onto the hope that he's just away on a business trip, and he'll be walking through the door any moment. I constantly search for him, instinctively reaching for the phone to share an amusing moment with him when the boys say something funny. The sound of a text message notification still tricks me into thinking it might be him. Even when I hear the garage door open, I catch myself thinking, "Collin is home."

But when I walked into the church and saw it adorned with flowers and photos of Collin, it was like I was realizing for the first time that he truly was gone. The weight of that realization hit me with so much intensity and force that I lost all control. In the rawness of my sorrow, every ounce of strength I had mustered to hold myself together crumbled in an instant. I felt utterly disoriented, unable to make sense of the flood of emotions washing over me. Numbness enveloped me, leaving me lost in a haze of heartbreak and disbelief.

I sprinted into the bathroom and allowed myself to let it all out. By the time the guests arrived, I had pulled myself together. As the service began, I sat in the front row with our boys, sandwiched between my parents and Collin's mother, with the rest of our extended family in the rows directly behind us.

Kelli spoke first, honoring Collin with a beautiful eulogy filled with love and pride. Her words echoed the depth of loss we all feel, yet also served as a testament to the enduring impact Collin had on the lives of those around him.

Then it was my turn to speak. With trembling hands and a heart heavy with emotion, I approached the chapel podium, knowing that this would be my final opportunity to honor him in this way. Laughter and tears intermingled as I recounted stories about Collin, the family we created, and our adventures together. I spoke of Collin's resilience, his courage in the face of adversity, and the unconditional love he had for God and his family.

These are some of the words I shared:

"When Collin was first diagnosed with leukemia in January 2021, we were, of course, devastated. But Collin had so much courage and assured me that everything would be okay. He prayed and pleaded with God and had many spiritual experiences. We witnessed miracle after miracle as Collin's life continued to be prolonged repeatedly. He felt and heard angels minister to him; he never lost his faith, he never doubted God's love for him.

For 559 days, he struggled and suffered in a diseased body. He endured more pain than any person should have to endure, and he did it with a smile! Never did he utter a word of complaint. Never did he get angry or bitter. And, he never gave up. Enduring to the end is the greatest and last earthly lesson Collin gave to our children.

Every day in the hospital, the doctors would come in and ask Collin how he was feeling. And almost every single time he would smile and say with enthusiasm, 'I feel good!' Of course, they knew that wasn't true, and they would turn to me and say, 'How is he really feeling?' Even when Collin felt his worst, he would take time to talk to all hospital staff to learn about them and their interests and hobbies; he would learn about their families. Collin is just good to the core, and he loves people! Everywhere we went, he would make friends. Usually, this made me and the boys crazy! But sometimes I would just sit back and watch in awe as my husband would make every person he came in contact with feel special.

One of Collin's favorite things to do was to travel with our family. It was important to him that the boys learn about cultural and social differences. He wanted them to appreciate the beauty of this earth and to gain life lessons from the experiences we had on our trips. Now, Collin, being a social butterfly, always amazed me with how many friends he would make on vacation.

We would be on a random beach or exploring a local town, and as we passed by people, he would wave at total strangers. 'Hi, Fred! Hey, Mary! How did it go last night, Doug?' And I would always be so confused and ask, 'How do you know that person?' I had never seen them before; to me, they were strangers. And he would nonchalantly say, 'Oh, that's my new buddy; I just met him yesterday, or I just met them today, and they are from Milwaukee, and they are here for their daughter's wedding.'

He would tell me who they were, where they were from, what they did for work, and why they were traveling. He just loved to mingle and loved everyone, and everyone loved him! I can honestly say I don't know one person who met Collin that didn't like him. He had a special way of making people feel important and loved. This was his superpower!

Collin and I made an incredible team. His strengths were my weaknesses, and my weaknesses were his strengths. Together, we made a perfect whole. We were perfectly imperfect. Collin and I knew each other better than we knew anyone else. We could finish each other's sentences, we knew each other's thoughts and desires; he is my best friend, and I can still feel him close.

The day he died; I asked him to promise to give me signs he was close by. I said, 'I need you to make them obvious, and I need them to be frequent. I need to know you are near.' He had lost his ability to speak, but he heard my plea and nodded his head. And I can tell you, he has kept that promise. He is near me, and although I can't physically see him, I can feel him. I still talk to him out loud, and he replies by putting thoughts into my mind. This is such a cherished gift! Our boys have also had their own experiences with their dad since he passed. They know he is watching over them; he is proud of them, and no doubt he will continue to guide and teach them until one day they are reunited with their amazing father.

Up until the very end, Collin believed with all his heart that he would be healed. Three weeks ago, the CAR-T cells that we all hoped would be the miracle that Collin so badly needed started to fail. Fear and anguish paralyzed my soul. Unlike me, Collin was not afraid. He confided that the Spirit had revealed to him that he no longer had to bear this burden and that he would indeed be healed. While this revelation brought him solace and me a measure of comfort, I couldn't help but question, 'Does this mean you will be healed in the next life?' Yet Collin was resolute. He insisted that his work on this earth was not finished and that he would be healed in this life. He believed he would be allowed to stay. That miracle did not come as we had hoped.

But Collin was not mistaken. He was healed, and his work on this earth is far from over. Death is not the end; Collin's spirit endures, and his legacy of courage, strength, faith, dedication, and love for his family and the Lord will continue to touch countless lives. I believe this with all my heart. I know the veil between our world and the spirit world is very thin. Though his spirit is no longer housed within his body, he still exists. We are separated only by a thin veil, allowing us to continue feeling his presence and communicate with him.

Our love story continues, and one day our family will be reunited, living together for eternity. In God's plan, there are no true endings, only everlasting beginnings. Until that joyous day, my love remains with you, echoing through the boundless expanse of time. I love you, Babe...until we meet again."

July 28, 2022

Today marks two weeks since Collin passed. The pain I feel is indescribable. Grief consumes me emotionally, mentally, and physically, often leaving me paralyzed. Collin fought for his life, and now it's my turn to fight for mine. The thought of a future without him is daunting; darkness swallows me whole. How am I supposed to navigate this despair? I'm uncertain, but I have to believe that I will figure it out.

As uncomfortable as it is to embrace the pain that grief causes, I realize that it's the only way to move forward. I don't hide my grief, and I'm not ashamed of it. Sometimes, our boys find me curled up and sobbing in a quiet room. No words are exchanged; they simply know what I need. They sit with me and offer comforting hugs. After a short time, the tears wash away the wave of emotions, and I find the strength to pick myself up and carry on.

Life continues, and I refuse to succumb to sorrow. Our children are looking to me for guidance on how to navigate through this. Every fiber of my being hates this new reality, but I cannot stay in bed all day, hoping for moments of joy to find me. I must actively seek them out to show myself and our sons that there are still reasons to enjoy living.

To honor Collin, these past couple of weeks we've immersed ourselves in activities he loved, finding comfort and joy in each adventure. From tubing the springs, kayaking the intracoastal, and shark fishing at night, to water parks, fireworks, bike rides, and indulging in plenty of beach time and delicious food, each moment has been a tribute to his vibrant spirit. These experiences have been both healing and heart-wrenching, underscoring the magnitude of our loss.

I've had to put forth a concerted effort to push myself forward, and it hasn't been easy. The weight of my grief feels unbearable, leaving me drained and lacking in motivation. Therefore, amidst all the activity, I am allowing myself plenty of scheduled periods of rest and introspection.

Despite drowning in this sea of grief, I remain resolute in my commitment to uphold Collin's legacy. His capacity to love and live fully inspires me to carry his essence forward with every step I take. In his memory, I embrace each day with determination, finding solace in the enduring presence of his spirit and the continued love and bond we share.

July 30, 2022

Throughout Collin's journey with cancer, he had many spiritual experiences. However, amidst his trials, he received revelations, one of which was particularly unexpected: he believed I would write a book about our story, specifically our story relating to his battle with cancer.

The first time Collin shared this revelation with me was in February 2021, and I couldn't help but laugh. After all, it hadn't been revealed to me. He must have been mistaken. I even joked, suggesting that he was meant to write the book, not me. But Collin remained adamant, it was to be me, not him. I dismissed his idea as a grand, whimsical notion. Yet, he persisted, gently nudging me every few months, inquiring about the book's content, title, and beginnings. My response was always the same, I had no desire to write a book.

Despite his persistence, I remained skeptical. I questioned who would want to read a book about cancer from my perspective when I wasn't the one battling the disease. But Collin, with his trademark smile, reassured me, "You just don't know it yet, but you are going to write a book." I can't recall the last conversation we had about the book, but it has been at least a few months, and to be honest, I had nearly forgotten about it.

Yet today, while biking the familiar trails near our home, I found myself in conversation with Collin, as I often do. I poured out my thoughts, fears, and doubts to him, the book being the furthest thing from my mind.

Unexpectedly, out of nowhere, these words clearly entered my mind: "The title of the book is A Million Miracles, and The One That Never Came." At that moment, I couldn't help but laugh at Collin's persistence. A single tear rolled down my cheek as I finally heard the call. I guess I'm going to write a book.

Conclusion

Collin's battle with leukemia and untimely death has left a gaping hole in my heart and soul. This experience has ripped me wide open, tearing apart my life, my future, and everything we had built together. His passing has affected every shard of my existence, leaving nothing untouched. With his death came the death of countless other things—our plans, dreams, hopes, vision, future, and the life we once knew—all shattered.

Despite the immense pain of his absence, our sons and I have been driven by the promise we made to Collin that his death would not diminish our light and love for life. Travel was always a priority for Collin and me. We had a shared passion for exploration and embarking on adventures together as a family was something that brought us immense joy. After his passing, the boys and I were determined to continue this tradition, honoring Collin's memory as we journeyed forth into the unknown.

Just six weeks after Collin left this earth, our sons and I embarked on our first international trip without him. It felt like a daunting undertaking, with the absence of his presence palpable every step of the way. However, amidst the mix of emotions, we discovered something profound: joy and pain can coexist in the same heart. Our journey was bittersweet, marked by moments of exhilaration intertwined with profound sadness. Yet, through it all, we felt Collin's spirit beside us, infusing each new experience with his adventurous energy. Ultimately, the trip provided some healing to our grieving hearts.

As the days and months went by, I felt haunted by memories of Collin and our time together; they were painful reminders of what I no longer possessed. It felt like robbery, leaving me utterly powerless. I yearned for his presence, desperately wishing for things to return to what I once deemed as "normal". But the reality is that his death had fundamentally altered my perspective, challenged my beliefs, and reshaped my identity.

A few months after Collin died, I recall staring into the mirror and feeling so disconnected from the person in the reflection, as if I were gazing upon a stranger. For 23 years, I had envisioned myself as part of a team with my husband, a dynamic duo. However, when I lost him, I lost countless pieces of myself too. Uncertainty about who I was and where I belonged in the world accompanied these thoughts, along with a pervasive sense of fear.

As I continue to press forward, I gradually search for and collect those tiny pieces of my identity. Some I find, and with amazement, I realize they still fit! I gently put them back into place, and this brings me comfort and familiarity. Yet, there are pieces I must acknowledge no longer fit; and as much as it hurts, I must let them go. Here's the thing I've come to realize: one's identity is not meant to be static—it's fluid, constantly evolving. Instead of viewing my identity as something fixed and unchanging, I choose to see it as a living, breathing entity—one that continues to grow and evolve. Embracing the idea that I am a work in progress has allowed me to release the pressure of trying to get back to normal and instead lean into the process of becoming.

After Collin took his last breath, I sought solace in grief therapy, attending sessions with unwavering commitment. I consumed a library's worth of grief books, hungry for healing and understanding, and diligently followed every piece of advice offered to me. Yet, despite my efforts and the outward appearance of progress, my life felt empty, devoid of the vibrant colors that once painted my world. Sure, there were fleeting moments of joy, but mostly every day seemed like a gray-scale version of what life used to be, a never-ending cycle of emptiness that threatened to suffocate me.

I recall a conversation with my therapist, who praised my supposed progress. But deep down, I questioned, "Is this what healing looks like? I feel so lost. I don't want to live like this for the next 40, 50, 60 years." It was a soul-crushing realization. But I refused to settle for a life devoid of true happiness. The prospect of enduring this desolation for decades ahead was unbearable.

Determined to not just survive but thrive, I enrolled in a Life Coaching School to become certified as a life coach. I was not too familiar with life coaching, but I felt that I had exhausted other traditional avenues, and therapy was not helping much. When I spoke with the enrollment counselor, I explained that my motivation for certification was to coach myself through life after loss. My goal was to reconnect with genuine joy and rediscover a life I loved. I made it clear that I had no intention of coaching anyone other than myself.

However, as I immersed myself in various coaching methods, techniques, and tools and applied them to my life alongside my knowledge and experience with grief, I underwent a profound transformational shift. It felt as if lightning had struck, illuminating a path forward. For the first time in three years, I felt a surge of empowerment, as if an inner fire had ignited, driving me to seize control of my life with newfound determination and purpose.

I could not help but wonder, why isn't everyone teaching this? And with that thought, I realized I could not keep this profound insight to myself. It became clear to me that I had a calling to help others navigate the impossible journey of life after loss, and ultimately, find healing.

I never expected that, amidst the depths of sorrow, I would discover a purpose to my pain. With this epiphany, RISE with grief was born—a coaching business devoted to supporting grievers on their path toward healing and transformation.

My coaching practice, which is rooted in cognitive behavioral science, includes offering grief education, practical tools, and insights to my clients. As I work closely with them, the focus is not just on understanding the psychological and physical aspects of grief but also on uncovering what's holding them back. My goal is to guide them toward finding hope, peace, and joy again, all while honoring their loved ones and continuing their bond with them.

Launching RISE with grief has been both a challenging and rewarding endeavor. It has enabled me to channel my grief into something meaningful, offering hope and support to others who are walking a similar path. As I guide grievers through their journey of healing, I am reminded of the resilience of the human spirit and the transformative power of love.

My life now looks quite different from the frantic pace of hospital stays, medical appointments, and the relentless pursuit of life-saving treatments. With Collin's passing, my world came to an abrupt halt. At first, the silence was deafening. The absence of urgency left an uncomfortable void, and I struggled to adjust to the newfound stillness. But gradually, I began to appreciate the beauty in the mundane. Grocery shopping, cooking meals, and tending to household chores became grounding rituals, anchoring me in the present moment and offering a sense of stability amidst the chaos of loss.

Today, I welcome the familiar routine of school drop-offs, sports practices, and bedtime stories, finding solace in the rhythm of normal daily life. I love simply being present with our sons, and I gain strength from their resilience. Together, we have learned to embrace the full spectrum of the human experience–the joy and the pain, the love and the loss. We understand healing is not a linear process, and though the ache may never fully subside, we take comfort in knowing that Collin's spirit lives on. His laughter echoes through the halls of our home, his presence is felt in the gentle breeze that rustles through the trees, and his love shines brightly in the eyes of our children. Collin's legacy continues and serves as a beacon of light in the darkness of loss.

I want to extend my gratitude to all who have supported Collin, myself, and our children on this challenging journey. To our family, friends, and community, I cannot express enough appreciation for your steadfast presence. Your kindness, empathy, and encouragement have provided us with strength and solace when we needed it most. We are profoundly grateful for your generosity, compassion, and willingness to walk alongside us as we navigate the complexities of grief and healing. Your companionship has made all the difference, and your constant love and solidarity have deeply touched us.

And to Collin, my beloved husband, thank you for your love and dedication to our family. I cherish our memories together; they continue to sustain me. Though you may be physically gone from this world, your life and legacy continue to guide us forward with love and light. As I navigate the ever-changing landscape of grief, I find comfort in knowing that our souls remain forever connected and that one day, we will be reunited. Your presence is palpable in every moment, reminding me that I am never truly alone.

Together, we rise.

ABOUT THE AUTHOR

Kelci Jager is a certified life coach, grief and loss coach, and registered nurse. As a widow and mother of four sons, Kelci brings a profound personal understanding to her professional work, allowing her to connect deeply with her clients facing life's challenges. With a passion for helping others, Kelci has dedicated her career to guiding individuals through personal transformation and healing.

As the founder of RISE with grief, Kelci combines her professional training and personal experiences to offer a unique approach to grief coaching. Her methodology focuses on empowering others to reclaim their joy and find new purpose after loss, without dismissing their pain. Kelci's coaching practice emphasizes resilience, personal growth, and the development of practical coping strategies. Her work has touched the lives of numerous individuals, providing support and guidance as they navigate their grief journey.

Kelci is also the author of "A Million Miracles and The One That Never Came," a book that complements her coaching work by offering readers insights into the journey of resilience and transformation.

To learn more about Kelci Jager's coaching services, workshops, and speaking engagements, or to explore how she can support your journey toward renewal and emotional well-being, visit RISEwithgrief.com.

Printed in Great Britain
by Amazon